Adobe Dreamweaver CS4

STEP BY STEP
TRAINING

↖ NOBLE DESKTOP

AUTHORIZED
Training Center
Adobe

Published by:
Noble Desktop LLC
594 Broadway, Suite 1202
New York, NY 10012
www.nobledesktop.com

ISBN: 978-1-934624-06-7

This book was typeset using Linotype Syntax Pro and printed and bound in the United States of America.

BONUS EXERCISES

REFERENCE MATERIAL

CD
INSTALLATION

Thank you for purchasing a Noble Desktop Course Workbook!

These instructions tell you how to install the class files used in this workbook.

Never open files directly from the CD — always copy the folders to your hard drive or you may get unexpected results!

(**HOW TO INSTALL CLASS FILES**)

1. Navigate to your hard drive (C: drive for Windows users) and make a **new folder** called **Class Files.**

2. Put the Class Files CD in your computer.

3. Open the CD, but **do not open any individual folders.**

4. Select all of the folders if there is more than one.

5. Drag them all into the **Class Files** folder you just made. These are the files you will use while going through the workbook.

6. Eject the CD.

   That's it! Enjoy.

WHAT IS HTML?

HTML stands for **Hypertext Markup Language.** It's a standardized system for tagging text-based information. HTML allows computers of various platforms— Mac, Windows, etc.—to view information in essentially the same way. It helps bridge the gap between the different computer systems people use.

Even though most users will see the information as you intended, it can appear differently based on the users' browser or operating system. For example, one person may see the text in Times, another sees Helvetica (because they uninstalled the Times font). While the webpage may not appear exactly the same to every user, the important thing is that all users have an acceptable experience and can access the content you provide.

WHAT IS CSS?

CSS stands for **Cascading Style Sheets.** It's a style language used to define the colors, fonts, etc. of elements in an HTML file. The main concept is that HTML files hold the content and CSS formats that content.

Because HTML and CSS are evolving languages, some users with older browsers may not be able to see effects that you include in your webpages. This is a factor to consider when designing webpages. For example, some newer CSS features may not work in a particular web browser. You have to ask yourself, can you live with the difference? If not, maybe there are only a few people using that browser so it won't be a problem. Maybe you should wait until more people use browsers that support the feature.

HTML TAGS

Information in HTML documents is surrounded by tags.
These tags are enclosed in less than (<) and greater than (>) brackets.
If you want a heading, for example, you need to specify it as:

```
<h1>This is My Heading</h1>
```

Note that the heading is followed by a closing tag </h1>. Most HTML tags require this ending or closing tag. If you have problems while programming HTML documents—for example, you cannot display a table correctly—it may be because you forgot to end the table with the </table> tag.

Most tags have closing tags. However, some may work even if you don't include the end tag. For example, the <p> tag, which indicates a new paragraph (and the space below it), often works without a closing </p>. Of course you should use the closing tag to ensure it works properly in all browsers. Other tags do not have closing tags at all, such as <img> (image) and
 (linebreak).

HTML tags are not case sensitive, but some things such as filenames and CSS style names are. In general, it is best practice to write all tags in lower case.

GRAPHIC FILES

There are three main graphic file formats you can use on the web. One format is GIF (Graphic Interchange Format). GIF compression limits the number of colors in an image to a maximum of 256, and works well for illustrations that are more flat and solid. While the numbers of colors are limited, GIF compression does **not** actually reduce image quality.

PNG compression is a lot like GIF. It also works best on flat, solid artwork, but files are often up to 25% smaller. Unlike GIF, PNGs can support semi-transparency.

The third format is JPEG (Joint Photographic Experts Group). JPEG compression supports millions of color and is particularly good for photographic images, because it can compress files without much obvious loss in quality. More compression yields a smaller file, but also creates more visible artifacts, such as loss of detail and the appearance of unsightly square blocks.

Regardless of the physical pixel density on a monitor, all computers display images at 72 pixels per inch. Therefore all web graphics should be 72 **ppi** (and RGB color).

NAMING FILES

- When naming files, HTML documents should end with the extension **.html** or **.htm** (It doesn't matter which extension, but you should stay with it once you've decided on a standard.)

- The homepage of a website should be named **index.html** (or **index.htm**).

- Graphics files should end in **.gif** if GIF files, **.png** for PNG file, and **.jpg** if JPEG files.

DOWNLOADING THE LATEST BROWSERS

All browsers handle code slightly differently, so as a web developer it's important to have all the current popular browsers installed for testing purposes. Below are links to download the most recent version of the browsers. Windows comes with Internet Explorer, so you should download Firefox and Safari. Macs come with Safari, so you should download Firefox. Internet Explorer for the Mac is no longer being developed or distributed.

Firefox: http://www.firefox.com   **Safari:** http://www.apple.com/safari

REFERENCE

ADDING A BROWSER TO DREAMWEAVER'S LIST

If a web browser doesn't appear in Dreamweaver's **Preview in Browser** menu, here's how to add it.

1. In Dreamweaver go to **Edit > Preferences** (WINDOWS) or **Dreamweaver > Preferences** (MAC).

2. Click **Preview in Browser** on the left.

3. Click the plus button (+) and you'll get the **Add Browser** dialog.

4. Click **Browse…** and choose the web browser (such as **Firefox)**.

5. If desired, edit the **Name** and click **OK.**

6. Click **OK** again to close the Preferences dialog.
   The new browser will now appear when you go to **File > Preview in Browser.**

INTRODUCTION TO HTML & CSS CODING

Coding HTML & CSS in Dreamweaver's Code View

Required HTML Tags

Inline CSS Styling

CODING TEXT FORMATTING

Headings

Alignment

Paragraphs & Line Breaks

Bold & Italic

Font Face

Font Size

Text Color and Background Color

Lists: Bulleted, Numbered

HORIZONTAL RULES

LINKS

Linking to Other Pages within You Website

Linking to External Websites

(metatags for search engines)

title appears in titlebar ← <head>
Filename becomes URL.

<u><body> .... </body></u>

<p> </p> - paragraph tabs.

<h#>   h1-h6   - 6 levels of headings   2 lines above + below
                  - accessible to visually impaired -
<b> ← <strong>
          - Bold text format   } Combining :
<i> ← <em>
          - italics (emphasis)   <b><i> .... </i></b>
                                              (Nesting Tags !!)

              line

      break   - doesn't need a closing tab.
          (soft return)

Front End Development (vs Backend - database)

Cmd O - open
N - new

EXERCISE OVERVIEW

To get started with this book, you'll need to do a little setup first. It is very important that you do this exercise, or some things later in the book will not work correctly!

SETTING UP YOUR OWN COPY OF CLASS FILES

Throughout this workbook you will be editing class files that we have prepared for you. Instead of the editing the originals, we'll have you make a copy just for yourself to edit.

1. If you are in Dreamweaver, minimize or hide it so you can see the Desktop.

2. Follow the appropriate Windows or Mac instructions below:

   (WINDOWS): Go into **My Computer > C: Drive > Class Files.**
   - Click once on the **Dreamweaver Class** folder to select it.
   - Press **Ctrl–C** to copy it.
   - Press **Ctrl–V** to paste it.
   - The new copy may be at the bottom of the list of folders.
     Rename it **yourname-Dreamweaver Class.**

   (MAC): Go into your **Hard Drive > Class Files.**
   - Click once on the **Dreamweaver Class** folder to select it.
   - Press **Cmd–D** to duplicate it.
   - Rename the duplicate folder to **yourname-Dreamweaver Class.**

3. You now have your own set of class files to use throughout the class. Have fun!

CUSTOMIZING PREFERENCES

Before we begin working in the program, we will have you modify the preferences to make the program a little friendlier and to make sure Dreamweaver is coding the proper version of HTML. These steps are very important.

1. Launch **Dreamweaver.**

2. Go into **Edit > Preferences** (WINDOWS) or **Dreamweaver > Preferences** (MAC).

3. On the top left of the window that appears click on the **General** category.

4. On the right side, near the top, make sure **Show Welcome Screen** is UNchecked.

5. On the left of the window click the **New Document** category.

6. Make sure the Default extension is set to **.html**

1A

EXERCISE

Setting Up For Class: Do This Exercise First! **DREAMWEAVER CS4**

7. Set the Default Document Type (DTD) to **HTML 4.01 Transitional.**

   NOTE: Dreamweaver defaults to have new documents use XHTML instead of standard HTML. The end result for the user is the same, but HTML is friendlier to code so we'll use it in class.

8. Finally, on the left of the window click the **Preview in Browser** category.

9. Under Options at the bottom make sure **Preview using temporary file** is **checked.** Now you won't get a pesky message asking to save the file every time you preview!

10. Click **OK** to get out of Preferences.

   (**SETTING THE WORKSPACE**)

1. Go to **Window > Workspace Layout > Classic.**

2. Go to **Window > Workspace Layout > Reset 'Classic'.** This resets the workspace to the default layout.

3. If you have the **Application Bar** turned on **(Window > Application Bar),** you should dock it to the right of the **Insert** panel.

Drag from here...   **...to here, and release when you see the blue line appear.**

4. Go to **File > Exit** (WINDOWS) or **Dreamweaver > Quit Dreamweaver** (MAC) and then relaunch the program. This will ensure that all the new preferences will be applied.

EXERCISE PREVIEW

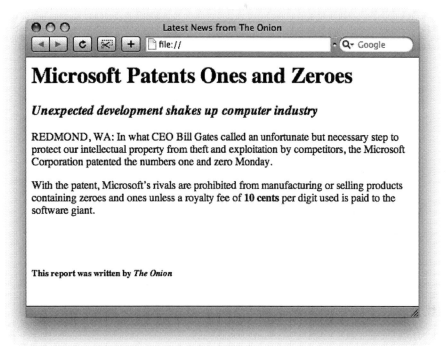

EXERCISE OVERVIEW

This first exercise is about as simple as it gets. Here you'll learn the very basics of HTML — bringing in some text, sizing it, adding the title, and making bold and italic text.

GETTING STARTED

1. Go to **File > Open**. *Cmd O*

2. Navigate to the **C: drive** (WINDOWS) or **Hard Drive** (MAC) and go into the **Class Files** folder, then **yourname-Dreamweaver Class** folder, then **News Website**.

3. Choose **microsoft.html** and click **Open**.

4. In the upper left corner, click the **Code** tab to switch into Code view. We'll use Code view for the rest of the HTML/CSS coding exercises. Later we'll use the other views.

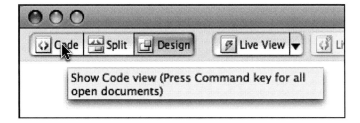

EXERCISE

5. We've typed out some text, but it doesn't have any HTML tags yet! Add the following **bold** code. (Line numbers are for reference only. Do not type them!)

   NOTE: Don't be alarmed when you type **</** to enter a closing tag, and Dreamweaver automatically enters the rest of the tag name. It usually does a good job, but always double-check that it's correct.

   ```
   1. <html>
   2. <head>
   3. <title>Latest News from The Onion</title>
   4. </head>
   5. <body>
   6. Microsoft Patents Ones and Zeroes
   7. Unexpected development shakes up computer industry
   8.
   9. REDMOND, WA: In what CEO Bill Gates called an unfortunate but
      necessary step to
   10. protect our intellectual property from theft and exploitation by competitors,
   11. the Microsoft Corporation patented the numbers one and zero Monday.
   12.
   13. With the patent, Microsoft's rivals are prohibited from manufacturing or selling
   14. products containing zeroes and ones unless a royalty fee of 10 cents per digit
   15. used is paid to the software giant.
   16.
   17.
   18. This report was written by The Onion
   19. </body>
   20. </html>
   ```

> ### CODE COMPLETION
>
> As you begin typing a tag, Dreamweaver displays a list of suggested tags based on the letters typed. If the tag is highlighted in the list, press **Enter** (WINDOWS) or **Return** (MAC) to quickly enter the rest of the word. Don't forget the closing bracket!

6. Do a **File > Save As.** Name it **yourname-microsoft-patent.html.** You must save it into the **News Website** folder as described below:

   (WINDOWS): At the top of the dialog box, under **Save in:** go to the **C: Drive.** Then open **Class Files,** then **yourname-Dreamweaver Class,** then **News Website,** then click **Save.**

   (MAC): On the left of the dialog box click **Desktop.** Then open the **Class Files** folder, then **yourname-Dreamweaver Class,** then **News Website,** then click **Save.**

7. Let's see what this page looks like now. Go to **File > Preview in Browser > and choose your favorite browser** to Preview the HTML page in that browser. If you're not sure, choose **Internet Explorer** (WINDOWS) or **Safari** (MAC).

8. The page will look like one long paragraph of text. Continue on to add some more formatting to the page.

HEADINGS

We want different text sizes for the headline and the subhead. We can do that with different Headings.

1. Add the following code highlighted in bold.

   ```
   5. <body>
   6. <h1>Microsoft Patents Ones and Zeroes</h1>
   7. <h3>Unexpected development shakes up computer industry</h3>
   ```

```
 8.
 9. REDMOND, WA: In what CEO Bill Gates called an unfortunate but necessary step to
10. protect our intellectual property from theft and exploitation by competitors,
11. the Microsoft Corporation patented the numbers one and zero Monday.
12.
13. With the patent, Microsoft's rivals are prohibited from manufacturing or selling
14. products containing zeroes and ones unless a royalty fee of 10 cents per digit
15. used is paid to the software giant.
16.
17.
18. <h5>This report was written by The Onion</h5>
```

2. Go to **File > Preview in Browser > and choose your favorite browser** to Preview the HTML page in that browser. Much better.

PARAGRAPHS & LINE BREAKS

The headings added some spacing, but not in the middle paragraphs. Even though there are paragraphs in the code, the browser doesn't know where the paragraphs start and end and where to add space. We'll have to tell it.

1. Add the following code highlighted in bold.

```
 9. <p>REDMOND, WA: In what CEO Bill Gates called an unfortunate but necessary step to
10. protect our intellectual property from theft and exploitation by competitors,
11. the Microsoft Corporation patented the numbers one and zero Monday.</p>
12.
13. <p>With the patent, Microsoft's rivals are prohibited from manufacturing or selling
14. products containing zeroes and ones unless a royalty fee of 10 cents per digit
15. used is paid to the software giant.</p>
16. <br>
17. <br>
18. <h5>This report was written by The Onion</h5>
```

2. Go to **File > Preview in Browser** to Preview the page.

BOLD & ITALIC

1. Add the following code highlighted in bold.

```
 6. <h1>Microsoft Patents Ones and Zeroes</h1>
 7. <h3><em>Unexpected development shakes up computer industry</em></h3>
 8.
 9. <p>REDMOND, WA: In what CEO Bill Gates called an unfortunate but necessary step to
10. protect our intellectual property from theft and exploitation by competitors,
11. the Microsoft Corporation patented the numbers one and zero Monday.</p>
12.
13. <p>With the patent, Microsoft's rivals are prohibited from manufacturing or selling
14. products containing zeroes and ones unless a royalty fee of <strong>10 cents</strong>
    per digit
15. used is paid to the software giant.</p>
16. <br>
17. <br>
18. <h5>This report was written by <em>The Onion</em></h5>
```

2. Go to **File > Preview in Browser** to Preview the page.

3. Very nice. Go to **File > Save.** Then leave it open so you can use it in the next exercise.

4. If you finish early, practice variations of the code, such as trying different
heading levels and experimenting with `<strong>` and `<em>` tags.

HTML TAGS INTRODUCED IN THIS EXERCISE

`<html></html>`	These tags enclose the entire document
`<head></head>`	Defines information about the HTML document
`<title></title>`	Encloses the title for the document which appears in the title bar
`<body></body>`	These tags completely enclose the main content for the document
`<h1></h1>...<h6></h6>`	Heading levels: **1** (main topic & largest size) to **6** (deepest subtopic & smallest size)
` `	Forces a line break
`<p></p>`	Defines a paragraph break
`<strong></strong>`	Enclosed content is rendered bold
`<em></em>`	Enclosed content is rendered italic

1C

Attributes - appears w/in bracket - modifies tags

eg. `<h1 ␣ align="center">`
    ‾‾‾‾‾‾‾‾‾
       attribute

`<tag ␣ attribute="value">`
      space

✗ Default alignment is left ✗

- Can have multiple attributes per tag separated by a single space

`<ul>` - bulleted list   or   `<ol>` ordered (numbered) list
(unordered list)

`<li>` - list item

eg. `<ul>`
    `<li> ... </li>`
    `<li> ... </li> ...`
    `</ul>`

eg. of bullet attributes: `type="circle"`

✗ spacing of #'s - more control in CSS ✗

EXERCISE PREVIEW

Some other patents that Microsoft owns:

- o Windows Vista
- o Microsoft Office
- o Xbox 360

EXERCISE OVERVIEW

HTML has a number of ways to display lists. Here you'll make a simple bulleted list. You can also try turning it into a numbered, ordered list.

CREATING A LIST

1. Modify the code from the previous exercise **(yourname-microsoft-patent.html)** to look like below. Changes are highlighted in bold. Carefully compare the code in our document to the code in yours.

   NOTE: Line numbers may not always match up exactly with what you type!

   ```
   13. <p>With the patent, Microsoft's rivals are prohibited from manufacturing or selling
   14. products containing zeroes and ones unless a royalty fee of <strong>10 cents</strong>
       per digit
   15. used is paid to the software giant.</p>
   16. <p>Some other patents that Microsoft owns:</p>
   17. <ul type="circle">
   18.    <li>Windows Vista</li>
   19.    <li>Microsoft Office</li>
   20.    <li>Xbox 360</li>
   21. </ul>
   22. <br>
   23. <br>
   24. <h5>This report was written by <em>The Onion</em></h5>
   ```

2. When finished, **Preview** it in a browser.

3. **Save** the file and leave it open so you can use it in the next exercise.

HTML ATTRIBUTES

Most HTML tags have attributes which are like preferences for that tag. They set options or change the behavior of a tag. For instance <h1> heading tags are aligned left by default, but we can change that to center with an attribute.

1. In the <h1> heading tag add `align="center"` as shown below:
   `<h1 align="center">Microsoft Patents Ones and Zeroes</h1>`

2. **Preview** it in a browser to see that the heading is now centered.

3. To change the heading to right aligned, in the code change **center** to **right.**

4. **Preview** it in a browser to see that the heading is now right aligned.

5. The heading looks best left aligned. Delete the `align="right"` so the code looks as follows: `<h1>Microsoft Patents Ones and Zeroes</h1>`

6. **Preview** it in a browser one last time to see that the heading is left aligned like it originally was.

```
EXPERIMENTATION (IF YOU HAVE EXTRA TIME)
```

1. Feel free to experiment by changing the **type** of the list to those listed in the reference below. You can also try converting the `<ul>` to an `<ol>` to change the bulleted list to a numbered list. Don't forget to change both the start and end tags!

2. **Save** the file and leave it open so you can use it in the next exercise.

HTML TAGS INTRODUCED IN THIS EXERCISE	
`<ul></ul>`	Unordered list that produces bulleted lists of items
	(type="square") attribute uses square bullets
	(type="circle") attribute uses open circles as bullets
	(type="disc") attribute uses solid circles as bullets
`<ol></ol>`	Ordered list that numbers the elements in order of occurrence
	(type="1") attribute uses numbers to order the list
	(type="a") attribute uses letters to order the list
`<li></li>`	Defines a single list item when using `<ol>` or `<ul>`

ID   CSS allows you to format typeface, color, size, pg background color etc.

Syntax different then HTML

(HTML w/ CSS)   ⟨tag ⌣ style = "property : value; ⌣ property : value;"⟩   Always ends
                                                    ↑ Not mandatory   w/ ;

Font family — list of fonts in case user does not
                have that 1ˢᵗ font → 2ⁿᵈ font ...

Color values —   # 000000 = black   # FFFFFF = white
                   ‾‾‾‾‾   ⌣ ⌣⌣
                  6 #'s or digits   R G B

        DW offers "websafe" color palette (256 colors)
                        ⌐ but very old. People have millions of colors now
          # 666633 — html → css # 663

EXERCISE PREVIEW

handwritten notes:
bckgrnd color
Style="background-color:#CCC;
color:#006; ← text color
font-size:12px;
Default is 16px (12pt)
Apply style to an area:
<span, style,...)
Can NEST

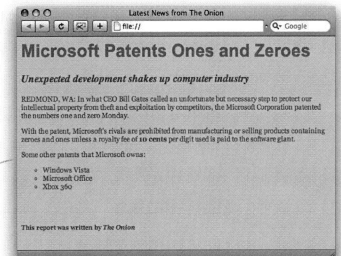

EXERCISE OVERVIEW

Now let's add some style to this page with some fonts and colors. We'll use CSS (Cascading Style Sheets) to do it. CSS is now the standard for styling web pages and this exercise gets you started with them.

1. Modify the code from the previous exercise **(yourname-microsoft-patent.html)** to look like below. Changes are highlighted in bold. Carefully compare the code in our document to the code in yours. NOTE: Line numbers may not always match up exactly with what you type.

```
1.  <html>
2.  <head>
3.  <title>Latest News from The Onion</title>
4.  </head>
5.  <body style="background-color:#CCCCCC; color:#666666;">
6.  <h1 style="font-family: Arial, Helvetica; color:#0075A4;">Microsoft Patents Ones and
    Zeroes</h1>
7.  <h3><em>Unexpected development shakes up computer industry</em></h3>
8.  <span style="font-family: Georgia, Times; font-size: 13px;">
9.  <p>REDMOND, WA: In what CEO Bill Gates called an unfortunate but necessary step to
10. protect our intellectual property from theft and exploitation by competitors,
11. the Microsoft Corporation patented the numbers one and zero Monday.</p>
12.
13. <p>With the patent, Microsoft's rivals are prohibited from manufacturing or selling
14. products containing zeroes and ones unless a royalty fee of <strong>10 cents</strong>
15. per digit used is paid to the software giant.</p>
16. <p>Some other patents that Microsoft owns:</p>
17. <ul type="circle">
18.   <li>Windows Vista</li>
19.   <li>Microsoft Office</li>
20.   <li>Xbox 360</li>
21. </ul>
22. <br>
23. <br>
24. <h5>This report was written by <em>The Onion</em></h5>
25. </span>
26. </body>
27. </html>
```

handwritten notes: don't need space

handwritten note: but h5 overwrites span

htm vs html - no difference (ask Co.)

NOTE: Any time you enter an attribute that calls for a color, Dreamweaver will display a color picker. Click on the desired color and Dreamweaver will enter the hexadecimal equivalent for you. Awesome!

2. When completed, **Preview** in the browser.

3. **Save** the file and leave it open so you can use it in the next exercise.

HTML AND CSS INTRODUCED IN THIS EXERCISE	
`<span></span>`	(HTML) Used as a wrapper for content. By itself, this tag does nothing. Typically a style attribute is added to format the content inside.
`style="property:value;"`	An HTML attribute used to apply CSS styling.
`font-family`	(CSS) Sets font family. The first font will be used if available. The second, third, etc. font will only be used if the proceeding font is not available.
`font-size`	(CSS) Sets text size. Most people specify in pixels (px) because they are more consistent and easiest to understand.
`color`	(CSS) Sets text color. Specified as a hexadecimal value. **Do not forget the # in front!**
`background-color`	(CSS) Sets background color of an element. Specified as a hexadecimal value. **Do not forget the # in front!**

properties (handwritten annotation bracketing font-family, font-size, color, background-color)

IE

Call your homepage: index.html

Files all lowercase + no spaces.
  └ use - or _ (ask Co.)

Root folder for all contents of your site
Local Root folder - your desktop
Remote Root folder - sent to server

Dead Ends are not good for websites

Should always test in multiple browsers   *IE6, IE7 (IE8 beta)*
        IE testing ← google   *IE, Firefox + Safari*

Intel MAC- run windows on your MAC.   *Bootcamp or Parallels. $80*
                                              allows run. windows same time
        or use your old PC

EXERCISE PREVIEW

computer industry

fortunate but necessary step to protect our competitors, the Microsoft Corporation *paten*

manufacturing or selling products contai git used is paid to the software giant.

Link to a file or an external URL

`<a href= "http://www.____.com"`

EXERCISE OVERVIEW

What would a web page be without links? You'll hand code a few links here to learn how it's done.

1. Modify the code from the previous exercise (**yourname-microsoft-patent.html**) to look like below. Changes are highlighted in bold.

```
 8. <span style="font-family: Georgia, Times; font-size: 13px;">
 9. <p>REDMOND, WA: In what CEO Bill Gates called an unfortunate but necessary step to
10. protect our intellectual property from theft and exploitation by competitors,
11. the <a href="http://www.microsoft.com" target="_blank">Microsoft Corporation</a> patented
    the numbers one and zero Monday.</p>
12.
13. <p>With the patent, Microsoft's rivals are prohibited from manufacturing or
14. selling products containing zeroes and ones unless a royalty fee of
15. <strong>10 cents</strong> per digit used is paid to the software giant.</p>
16. <p>Some other patents that Microsoft owns:</p>
17. <ul type="circle">
18.   <li>Windows Vista</li>
19.   <li>Microsoft Office</li>
20.   <li>Xbox 360</li>
21. </ul>
22. <p>Wall Street reacts to MS Patent News. <a href="wall-street.html">Read more...</a></p>
23. <br>
24. <br>
25. <h5>This report was written by <em><a href="http://www.theonion.com" target="_blank">
    The Onion</a></em></h5>
26. </span>
```

2. When finished, **Preview** it in a browser and click the links to confirm they work.

3. **Save** the file.

HTML TAGS INTRODUCED IN THIS EXERCISE

`<a></a>` Anchor	Sets enclosed content as a hypertext link	
`(href)`	attribute specifies the location of the link	
`(target= "_blank")`	attribute specifies that the link will open in a new window.	

Images: Optimize images for the web. — Photoshop
                                                Illustrator (logos)

Fireworks (replaces ImageReady in Photoshop)

        Best File format   JPEG - has more colors.

            pixel wth.

                            Quality - how many pixels. Less quality =
                                                         smaller file size

Gif good for animation or transparencies. PNG for transparencies (PNG 8 for web)
JPEG- solid white background   lower file size by lower # colors

In Photoshop - "save for web + other devices." Don't save as jpeg - to heavy

_____

2B   Tables   tag: <table> </table>

<table>
    <tr>   table row
    <td>   column (table data) — Contents go inside td's
                                                        for gutter
                                                      / around content

tablu spec :

        <table border ="1" width="650" bgcolor="color" align="center" cellpadding="1"

                                    attribute gets set for
                                    entire column
                                          table
ex. <tabu>
        <tr>
            <td>... </td>   } 1 row, 3 olumns
            <td>... </td>
            <td>... </td>
        <tr>
    </table   tr should nver get an attribute

        Merge columns: colspan = "#g columns"

                        rowspan

        Vertical alignment: valign="top"   } default middle
                                      "bottom"
                                                                    cellpodding:
        Bkgnd color for each cell : bgcolor = "...."   w/in cell.
        Cell Margins - default to 1px . cellspacing ="0" to remove

[handwritten: <!-- ... --> for Comments - makes invisible button to make comment on toolbar]

DREAMWEAVER CS4 *[handwritten: Corporate]*

Section Topics

SECTION 2

[handwritten: Resolution Default Std - 1024 x 768, 75 Hz, Millions]
[handwritten: Home User Std may be 800 x 600, 75 Hz, Millions]
[handwritten: Std width 974 safe. No Horiz. Scroll]

CODING IMAGES

GIF vs. PNG vs. JPEG
Image Attributes:
> *Alignment*
> *Horizontal & Vertical Space*
> *Borders*
> *Alt (Text Description for Images)*

TABLES

Using Tables to Lay Out a Page
Row and Column Spanning
Table Cell Alignment
Table Backgrounds

CASCADING STYLE SHEETS (CSS)

Tag Redefine Styles
Custom Styles (Class Styles)
Inline Styling

DREAMWEAVER DESIGN VIEW & INTERFACE

Insert Panel
Properties Panel

TEXT & PAGE FORMATTING

Text Formatting
Text Color
Formatting Lists
Webpage Background Color

DREAMWEAVER

Not embedding image   — images should be in a subfolder - image folder —
                                in Root folder

<img src="images/filename.jpg">

placement - put in own paragraph   <img ...>
                                            ↑
                                           div

when align is w/in img tag, get text wrap

Attributes :
                        ⌐ pixels
        vspace = "#"   } padding around
        nspace = "#"   }   image.

        height = "#"   } saves that exact space
        width = "#"   } for the image in case it loads
                               slowly or not at all.

        alt = "text"   — don't see text except if image doesn't load
                            or loads slowly (alternate text). Is
                            searchable.

            border = "#" pixel

    to make an image a link use anchor text around image tag
                    link border appears in firefox so
                    set border="∅"

EXERCISE PREVIEW

EXERCISE OVERVIEW

Images are another basic element of web page design. Here we'll show you how to add them to your page and control their location.

1. Go to **File > New** and set the following:
   - On the far left, choose **Blank Page.**
   - Page Type: **HTML**
   - Layout: **None**

   Click **Create.**

2. Notice the `<!DOCTYPE>` tag at the top? This tells the web browser to display the page according to a certain standard. It should be on every webpage to ensure the most consistency across browsers.

3. Do a **File > Save As.** Name it **yourname-bonnie.html** into the **News Website** folder.

4. Open the file **hurricane-text.html.** We've typed out the text to save you time.

5. Go to **Edit > Select All.**

6. Go to **Edit > Copy.**

7. Close the file and return to **yourname-bonnie.html.**

8. Place the cursor after the `<body>` tag and press **Enter** WINDOWS or **Return** MAC once.

9. **Edit > Paste** the text.

2A
EXERCISE

10. Insert the code highlighted in bold to get the following:

```
3.  <html>
4.  <head>
5.  <meta http-equiv="Content-Type" content="text/html; charset=UTF-8">
6.  <title>CNN Interactive</title>
7.  </head>
8.
9.  <body>
10. <img src="images/ad1.gif" width="120" height="60" alt="CNN Banner">
11. <img src="images/ad2.gif" width="468" height="60" alt="IBM Banner">
12. <hr size="1" noshade>
13. <h1>Bonnie weakens again,<br>
14. moving toward Nova Scotia</h1>
15. <img src="images/weathermap.jpg" width="197" height="201" border="2" align="right"
    alt="Radar Map of Hurricane Bonnie" hspace="20">
16. <h3>For now, Danielle is expected to stay clear of U.S. shores</h3>
17. <h5>August 29, 1998<br>
18. Web posted at: 1:25 p.m. EDT (1725 GMT)</h5>
19.
20. <p>(CNN) -- A fickle Hurricane Bonnie weakened into a tropical storm and
21. spiraled out to sea from the Virginia coast early Saturday.</p>
22. <p>At 5 a.m. EDT, Bonnie was about 635 miles (1,022 km) southwest of Sable
23. Island, Nova Scotia, and was moving northeast at about 17 mph (27 kmh).</p>
24. <p>Meanwhile, North Carolina residents were bracing for Bonnie's sister, Danielle.</p>
25.
26. </body>
27. </html>
```

11. **Save** the file.

12. **Preview** the page. Notice if you resize the window that the text wraps around the hurricane graphic. Also, if your window is too thin, the graphics at the top stack vertically underneath each other.

13. If you finish early, practice variations of the code such as trying out different alignment, border, and spacing options.

HTML TAGS INTRODUCED IN THIS EXERCISE

<img>	Places an image into the webpage
	(src) attribute designates the file name and location of the image
	(width) and **(height)** attributes define the image size
	(border) attribute sets a border around the image
	(align="left" or "right") attribute sets the image location
	(vspace) and **(hspace)** attribute adds space around the image
	(alt) attribute describes the image
<hr> (width)	attribute sets the width of the rule in pixels or percent (%) ~50% 100% default
horizontal rule	**(size)** attribute sets thickness of the rule in pixels 2px default
	(noshade) attribute removes the default shading
	(align="left" or "right") attribute sets the rule alignment. Default is **center**
	color = " colorpicker "

EXERCISE PREVIEW

EXERCISE OVERVIEW

This exercise shows you how to lay out a page using tables. Tables are one of the most common methods to organize content on a page.

1. Open the file **table.html** from the **News Website** folder.

2. Save it as **yourname-table.html.**

3. Look at the code, and then **Preview** it in a browser **(F12 (WINDOWS)** or **Opt–F12 (MAC)).**

4. Lines 11 through 15 are commented out. Delete the start and end of the comment (`<!-- -->`) on lines 11 and 15 (and delete the text **This is the start of a comment**).

5. To place the images in a new table row, with each image sitting in its own table cell, add the following bold code:

```
11. <tr>
12.     <td>
13.         <img src="images/newsthumb-patent-ones-n-zeros.jpg" alt="Microsoft Patents Ones
            and Zeros" width="190" height="145">
14.     </td>
15.     <td>
16.         <img src="images/newsthumb-hurricane.jpg" alt="Radar Map of Hurricane Bonnie"
            width="190" height="145">
17.     </td>
18.     <td>
19.         <img src="images/newsthumb-patent-wall-street.jpg" width="190" height="145">
20.     </td>
21. </tr>
```

6. **Preview** to see what the changes look like. You should now have a row of images on top of a row of text.

2B
EXERCISE

7. Put the cursor at the beginning of line **11**, press **Enter** (WINDOWS) or **Return** (MAC).

8. We want to add a new title at the top of the table. Starting in the empty line you just made, **add** this new code to create a table row. Do not edit the code that is already there, this is **new** code that you will type out.

```
11. <tr>
12.      <td colspan="3" style="font-family:Arial, Helvetica, sans-serif;
         font-size:24px; color:#FFFFFF;">
13.          <strong>Late Breaking News</strong>
14.      </td>
15. </tr>
```

9. **Preview** to see what it looks like.

ALIGNMENT AND SPACING

1. Looking better, but the heading would look better centered, and the three column widths are not equal. Add the **align**, **valign** and **width** attributes to the `<td>` tags to match the code below.

```
11. <tr>
12.      <td colspan="3" align="center" style="font-family:Arial, Helvetica, sans-serif;
         font-size:24px; color:#FFFFFF;">
13.          <strong>Late Breaking News</strong>
14.      </td>
15. </tr>
16. <tr>
17.      <td width="33%">
18.          <img src="images/newsthumb-patent-ones-n-zeros.jpg" alt="Microsoft Patents
             Ones and Zeros" width="190" height="145">
19.      </td>
20.      <td width="34%">
21.          <img src="images/newsthumb-hurricane.jpg" alt="Radar Map of Hurricane Bonnie"
             width="190" height="145">
22.      </td>
23.      <td width="33%">
```

2. The paragraphs in the last row should all be aligned to the top of their cells. Add **valign="top"** to the following three lines as shown in bold below.

```
28. <td valign="top">
29.      <span style="font-family:Arial, Helvetica, sans-serif; font-size:16px;

32. <td valign="top">
33.      <span style="font-family:Arial, Helvetica, sans-serif; font-size:16px;

36. <td valign="top">
37.      <span style="font-family:Arial, Helvetica, sans-serif; font-size:16px;
```

3. **Preview** to see what it looks like.

SPACING & BORDERS

1. Add **cellpadding** and **cellspacing** attributes to the `<table>` tag so it reads like this:

```
<table width="760" border="1" align="center" cellpadding="15" cellspacing="0">
```

2. **Preview** to see what it looks like.

3. Change the table's border attribute to **0**, so it looks like this:

```
<table width="760" border="0" align="center" cellpadding="15" cellspacing="0">
```

4. **Preview** to see what it looks like.

(ADDING SOME COLOR)

This table needs to stand out against the background.

1. Add a **bgcolor** attribute to the table (the code should be on one line).

```
<table width="760" bgcolor="#FFFFFF" border="0" align="center"
cellpadding="15" cellspacing="0">
```

2. **Preview** to see what it looks like.

3. Oh no! The header text is white too and now we can't read it.
Around line **12,** add a bgcolor attribute to the header's `<td>` tag.

```
<td colspan="3" bgcolor="#666666" align="center" style=
```

4. **Preview** one last time and smile.

5. Try experimenting with rows and columns. Add a new table row either on the
top or the bottom. If you really feel like a challenge, add a new table column to
the right.

6. When finished, **Save** and **Close** the file.

(EXTRA CREDIT (BONUS IF YOU HAVE SPARE TIME))

If you have extra time here is some more practice with tables.

1. Open the file **hurricane.html.**

2. Look at the code. You see that it is basically the same as a previous exercise.

3. **Preview** to see what it looks like (**F12** (WINDOWS) or **Opt–F12** (MAC)).

4. Resize the browser window to see how the page reacts. Notice when the
window is wide, the text and rule stretch all the way across. When the window
is thin, the text bunches up, and the graphics stack on top of each other. To
avoid this, we are going to place everything in a table.

5. Close the preview and switch back to Dreamweaver.

6. Just before the first `<img>` tag, add these three lines:

```
<body>
<table width="600" border="1" cellpadding="4" cellspacing="0">
<tr>
<td>
<img src="images/ad1.gif" width="120" height="60" alt="CNN Banner" border="0">
```

EXERCISE

7. To close the table, just above the end body tag `</body>` add these three lines:

```
</td>
</tr>
</table>
</body>
```

8. **Preview** to see what it looks like.

9. Now resize the window again. Notice that the layout is locked into a 600-pixel area.

    NOTE: Currently most web sites are designed for screen resolutions of 800x600 pixels or 1024x768 pixels:
    • For 800x600 screens a table width of 760 pixels will fit (750 is a little more conservative).
    • For 1024x768 screens a 984 pixel table would fit (974 to be more conservative).

10. To see the page without the border around the table, in line 10 change the **border** attribute to **0** in the `<table>` tag.

11. Now let's add a new table row. At the bottom, after the `</tr>`, add the following :

```
</tr>
<tr>
    <td align="center" bgcolor="#FFCC33">Brought to you by CNN</td>
</tr>
</table>
```

12. When you **Preview**, you will notice that the text is centered in a colored table.

13. Close the file and do not save the changes.

HTML TAGS INTRODUCED IN THIS EXERCISE

`<table></table>`	defines the start of a table
	(width) and **(height)** attributes define the size of the overall table
	this can be expressed in percentages or pixels
	(border) attribute sets a border around the table
	(cellpadding) attribute puts pixels of space around each cell
	(cellspacing) attribute puts pixels of space between each cell
`<tr></tr>`	creates a row within the table
`<td></td>`	creates a cell within the row
	(width) and **(height)** attributes define the size of the cell
	(align="left" or **"right"** or **"center")** attribute defines how cell contents are aligned horizontally
	(valign="top" or **"middle"** or **"bottom")** attribute defines how cell contents are aligned vertically
	(colspan) attribute defines how many columns the cell will span
	(rowspan) attribute defines how many rows the cell will span

EXERCISE PREVIEW

EXERCISE OVERVIEW

In this exercise you'll style the page using Cascading Style Sheets (CSS). CSS can automatically give all your headings and paragraphs a certain look or style.
In just a few simple steps this page will go from plain text, to colored styled text.

1. Go to **File > Open.**

2. Go to the **yourname-Dreamweaver Class** folder, then **AutomoTips.**

3. Choose the file named **used-car-shopping-tips.html** and click **Open.**

4. Do a **File > Save As.**

5. Rename it **yourname-used-car-shopping-tips.html** and save it back into the **AutomoTips** folder.

6. **Preview** the file so you can see how the original looks.
   Notice there are headings and paragraphs of text.

TAG REDEFINES (A GOOD WAY TO SET "DEFAULT" APPEARANCE)

There are three types of styles we are going to look at: HTML redefines, class styles, and inline styling. The first type will redefine the look of existing HTML tags to look differently.

1. Add the following new code in the `<head>` section to define the look of three styles. These styles redefine the look of the heading 1 and 2 and paragraph tags. They form a good basis for how the page will look. The code you must add is highlighted in bold:

```
<html>
<head>
    <title>AutomoTips: Used Car Shopping Tips</title>
<style type="text/css">
h1 {
    font-family: Arial, Helvetica, sans-serif;
    font-size: 25px;
    color: #E38000;
}
h2 {
    font-family: Arial, Helvetica, sans-serif;
    font-size: 19px;
    color: #E38000;
}
p {
    font-size: 13px;
    line-height: 19px;
    color: #666666;
}
</style>
</head>
<body>
```

2. **Preview** the page in a browser.

    You should see the headings and paragraphs have been changed. These styles redefine HTML tags to look different. But what about text that doesn't have a tag, or if we want one paragraph to look different? That's next.

CUSTOM STYLES (MAKE EXCEPTIONS TO THOSE DEFAULTS)

Custom styles can be placed on any tag and let you decide where you want to apply them.

1. Under the p style add the following code shown in bold. (Yes the dot before **highlight** is there on purpose, that is what makes it a custom style!)

```
p {
    font-size: 13px;
    line-height: 19px;
    color: #666666;
}
.highlight {
    color: #900000;
}
</style>
```

2. Now that the style is created, you must apply it (custom styles don't automatically apply themselves as Tag redefines do). To apply the style, find the following code (should be in line 42) and add the class tag shown in bold here:

```
<p class="highlight">When inspecting the car, check it all over:</p>
```

3. **Preview** in the browser and look for the red text.

APPLYING CUSTOM STYLES WHEN THERE IS NO TAG PRESENT

1. Go back to the code and around line 53, at the end of the paragraph that starts with **Once you have inspected**, you should find the text **Check these features:** (you may have to scroll right to see it). We want to style it, but there is no tag for us to apply the class attribute to. We will add a `<span>` tag, which doesn't do anything by itself, but will let us add the **class** attribute that will style the text. Add the code in bold as follows:

   ```
   <p>Once you have inspected the car completely, take it on a test drive.
   <span class="highlight">Check these features:</span></p>
   ```

2. **Preview** in the browser and scroll down to see the red text.

INLINE STYLING

In the browser preview, notice the white space above the top image. That image is supposed to sit snug against the top of the window. The space is caused by a default margin in the browser, we need to tell it to have no spacing. While we could redefine the body tag, it's just as easy to add the styling inline.

1. In line 28, add the following style to the `<body>` tag

   ```
   <body style="margin:0px;">
   ```

2. **Preview** in the browser.
   Yes! That's how the site is supposed to look.

3. When finished, **Save** and **Close** the file.

CSS CODE INTRODUCED IN THIS EXERCISE	
`.name {attributes}`	Defines a CSS class style and the formatting attributes of that style.
`class="name"`	An attribute added to HTML tags. It calls the name of a class style. Add this to any tag to apply a class style to its contents.

CSS style tag in head of document

```
<style type="text/css">
...
</style>
```

Declaring styles.

```
<style type="text/css">
    h2 {property:value; property:value...}
        eg  font-family:....;
            font-size; 24px;  etc.
```

1. redefine HTML tags
2. create a custom style (using a class selector):
3. Compound selectors (combines 1 & 2)

custom style:

• name
↑
important!

} applying ex. `<p class="custom stylename">`
└ eg. "highlight"

Custom styles overwrite

`<span class="highlight">`..... `</span>`

Can save all CSS style declarations in a separate CSS file
in doc `<link href="name of file.css" type="text/css">` ← in head of doc.

(Inline css styles great for HTML email?)
     Default margins around html page

Properties box - In Design view

page properties - can Δ defaults using CSS (Appearance(CSS))

     body, td, th { ← tables + th to take on these styles
     }

Modify   Targeted Rule: in line style
                        class custom style

View Rulers

EXERCISE PREVIEW

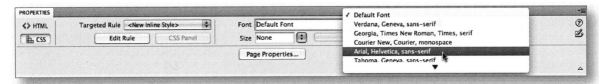

EXERCISE OVERVIEW

It's important to know HTML, but Dreamweaver can make coding web pages so much faster! Here we'll show you how to quickly format a basic page using Dreamweaver's Design View.

STYLING TEXT IN DESIGN VIEW

1. Go to **File > Open**.

2. Navigate to the **News Website** folder and choose **microsoft-styling.html**.

3. Do a **Save As** and name it **yourname-microsoft-styling.html**.

4. You are about to format the text to look like a previous exercise, but this time we'll use the design view and let Dreamweaver do the coding for us.

5. In the upper left corner, click the **Design** tab to switch into Design view.

6. You'll find text formatting options in the **Properties** panel at the bottom of the screen. If the **Properties** panel is not showing, go into **Window > Properties**.

   In CS4, Adobe divided the **Properties** panel into two sections, **HTML** and **CSS**. The sections format your page differently, using either HTML or CSS depending on what you want to use.

HTML PROPERTIES   PARAGRAPH FORMATTING   BOLD & ITALIC

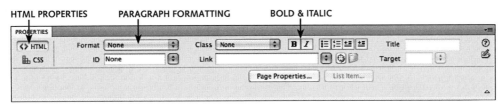

CSS PROPERTIES   HOW CSS STYLING IS APPLIED   FONT   TEXT ALIGNMENT

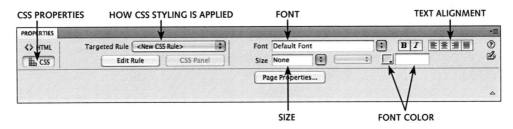

SIZE   FONT COLOR

7. Select the **first** line of text.

8. In the **Properties** panel, on the left side, press the **HTML** (<> HTML) button to make sure you are editing the HTML properties.

9. In the **Properties** panel change the **Format** to **Heading 1**.

10. Select the **second** line and make it:
    - Format: **Heading 3**
    - **Italic** (*I*)

11. Select the **last** line and change the **Format** to **Heading 5**.

12. Select the last two words **The Onion** and make them **Italic** (*I*).

13. Near the middle of the page, select the words **10 cents** and make them **Bold** (**B**).

14. As shown below, type in the title of the webpage in the **Toolbar** at the top of the window. Title it: **Latest News from The Onion**.
    (If you don't see the **Toolbar**, choose **View > Toolbars > Document**.)

15. Hit **F12** (WINDOWS) or **Option–F12** (MAC) to preview the page in the browser.

16. Go back to **Dreamweaver**. At the top left, click the **Code** (Code) button to switch to Code view and take a look at the HTML code of this webpage.

17. Wow, all that code so quickly!
    When you're finished, click the **Design** (Design) button to switch to design view.

ADDING COLOR & FONTS

1. Let's change the page's background color. Go into **Modify > Page Properties**.

2. On the left side, make sure you are in the **Appearance (CSS)** category.

3. Under **Background color**, type **#CCCCCC**, then click **Apply** to see the changes.

4. Under **Text color**, type **#666666**, then click **Apply** to see the changes.

5. On the left side, click **Links (CSS)** and set the following colors:
   - Link color: **#990000**
   - Visited links: **#0075A4**

   Click **Apply** to see the changes

6. On the left side, click **Headings (CSS)** and set the following:
   - **Heading font:** From the menu ( ) choose **Arial, Helvetica, sans-serif**
   - To the far right of **Heading 1** (just below the **B** button), type **#0075A4**

7. Click **OK** when done.

8. Dreamweaver CS4 added a **Code Navigator** which can be useful, when we want it. But it's icon (🔆) automatically appears next to your cursor after few seconds, so it often gets in the way. Let's disable it now. Go to **View > Code Navigator.**

9. In the document next to the cursor a panel will open. At the bottom right check on **Disable 🔆 indicator** if it's not checked already.

10. Click anywhere on the document outside the Code Navigator panel to close it.

11. At the beginning of the article, select the text **REDMOND, WA:**

12. In the **Properties** panel, on the left side, press the **CSS** (🟦 CSS) button to make sure you are editing the CSS properties.

13. Set the **Targeted Rule** to **<New Inline Style>.**

14. Under **Font,** choose **Arial, Helvetica, san-serif** from the menu (🔹).

FORMATTING A LIST

1. Select the three lines of text: **Windows Vista, Microsoft Office,** and **Xbox 360.**

2. In the **Properties** panel press the **HTML** (<> HTML) button to make sure you are editing the HTML properties.

3. Click the **Unordered List** (▤) button.

4. You should now have a bulleted list, but we'd like to change the type of bullets. Click anywhere in the **Windows Vista** line of text so the cursor is blinking there.

5. In the **Properties** panel click the **List Item** button.

6. From the **Style** menu choose **Square** and click **OK.**

7. You may remember from the coding exercise earlier in the workbook that we used a circle bullet, but that wasn't listed in Dreamweaver's style menu. Why is that? We aren't sure, but click the **Code** (⟨⟩Code) button at the top left of the window.

8. Find the **<ul>** tag and change: type="**square**" to type="**circle**"

9. Click the **Design** (⬚Design) button to see that Dreamweaver can even display the circle! While this is a rare exception to Dreamweaver's greatness, it is an example of how knowing HTML code gives you the ultimate power!

FINISHING UP

1. Put the cursor at the beginning of the last line of text.

2. Press **Enter** (WINDOWS) or **Return** (MAC) to add an empty paragraph of space.

3. That's a bit too much space, press **Backspace** (WINDOWS) or **Delete** (MAC).

EXERCISE

4. Now hold **Shift** and hit **Enter** ⟨WINDOWS⟩ or **Return** ⟨MAC⟩.
   This adds a line break
 (also called a soft return) instead of a full paragraph.

5. Preview the page by hitting **F12** ⟨WINDOWS⟩ or **Option–F12** ⟨MAC⟩.

6. Go back to **Dreamweaver** and open the **CSS Styles** panel
   (Window > CSS Styles).

7. At the top of the panel, click the **All** button to see all the styles. You will also
   probably need to click the **plus box** ⟨WINDOWS⟩ or **triangle** ⟨MAC⟩ next to **<style>** to
   see the full list. Dreamweaver uses CSS rules for most of the styling you do.

8. Switch to **Code** view and take a look at all the HTML tags and CSS rules
   that Dreamweaver painlessly created for you. Hurray, your coding days are
   over (mostly)!

9. Switch back to **Design** view then save and close the file.

3

PAGE LAYOUT

Using Tables to Lay Out a Page

LINKS

Linking to Other Pages within Your Website
Linking Up and Down within a Single Page
Linking to External Websites
Email Links

GRAPHICS

Images
Navigation Bars
Background Images

BEHAVIORS

Image Rollovers (Swap Image Behavior)

IMAGE MAPS

Creating and Linking Image Map Hotspots to Webpages
Adding Rollovers (Swap Image Behavior) to Image Maps

Preserve links use   Site > New Site → Site Definition window
                                          select Adv. tab.
                                      → Name the site name
                                        Local Root folder - browse +
                                                          select your Local
                                                          Root folder

EXERCISE PREVIEW

Things To Do

San Francisco is filled with culture, fine eating, night life and more. From beaches and parks, museums, bike riding, cable cars, to street performers, there is always something to do. The hard part is deciding how you'll spend your time! Here are a few recommendations:

Being on Alcatraz Island is a unique experience. There is an audio tour of the Cellhouse that is told be actual offices and inmates of Alcatraz. Tours run around 2.5 hours. Ticket prices range from $24.50–$31.50 for adults and $15.25–$18.75 for children (5–11). Toddlers (0–4) are free. The tour leaves from Pier 33 and is easily accessible by public transportation. After the tour, why not grab a bite to eat or do some shopping at Fisherman's Wharf? Back to Top

EXERCISE OVERVIEW

This is the first in a series of exercises where you'll lay out a complete website. The first step is to start laying out the basics of the page—we'll construct it with tables, then add text and images. Here we also introduce you to Site Management, which is a Dreamweaver feature that can help you maintain files across your whole site.

DEFINING A SITE

We have prepared a folder of files for you. This website folder contains images and some partially made webpages for you to finish. Let's tell Dreamweaver that this folder contains our website by defining a site.

1. In Dreamweaver choose **Site > New Site.**

2. In the **Site Definition** dialog that opens, click the **Advanced** tab at the top.

3. Next to **Site name** enter **yourname-Dianes Travels.**

4. Next to **Local root folder**, click on the folder (🗀) icon and navigate until you get to **Class Files.** Go into the **yourname-Dreamweaver Class** folder and

   (WINDOWS): Double-click on the subfolder **Dianes Travels.**
   Click the **Select** button.
   Click **OK** to finish defining the site.

   (MAC): Select the **Dianes Travels** folder and click **Choose.**
   Click **OK** to finish defining the site.

TABLES FOR LAYOUT

1. The **Files** panel should open towards the bottom right of the screen. (It can also be opened via **Window > Files.)** All files in our site folder appear in that **Files** panel. We'll use some of them later.

2. Go to **File > New.**
   - On the far left, choose **Blank Page.**
   - Page Type: **HTML**
   - Layout: **None**

   Then click **Create.**

3. Do a **File > Save As.**

4. Click the **Site Root** button at the bottom of the dialog. This puts you back into the **Dianes Travels** folder. (See sidebar for more explanation.)

5. Name the file **sanfran.html** and click **Save.**

6. At the top of the document window next to **Title** enter the following: **Diane's Travels - Because Travel is More Than Just Getting There**

7. The **Insert** panel should be visible at the top of the screen. If it is not, you can open it via **Window > Insert.**

8. Click the **Common** tab. These are objects that people commonly want to insert.

> **SITE ROOT EXPLAINED**
>
> When you have a site defined in Dreamweaver, you often want to quickly get to the main folder containing your website's files. This is called the root folder. Clicking the **Site Root** button is a fast way to go to this root folder.

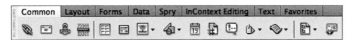

9. Click the **Table** (▦) button.

10. In the dialog that appears, put in these specs:

Rows: **1**	Columns: **2**
Table width: **750 (pixels)**	
Border thickness: **0**	
Cell padding: **12**	
Cell spacing: **0**	
Header: **None**	

    Leave the Accessibility options as is.
    Click **OK.**

11. With the table still selected, in the **Properties** panel change **Align** to **Center.**

12. In the **Files** panel, double-click the file **sanfran-text.html** to open it.

13. This is all the text for our page. **Select All** by pressing **Ctrl–A** ⓌⒾⓃⒹⓄⓌⓈ or **Cmd–A** ⓂⒶⒸ.

14. **Copy** it (**Ctrl–C** ⓌⒾⓃⒹⓄⓌⓈ or **Cmd–C** ⓂⒶⒸ).

15. Close the file.

16. You should now be back in **sanfran.html.**

17. Click in the right cell of the table and **Paste** (**Ctrl–V** ⓌⒾⓃⒹⓄⓌⓈ or **Cmd–V** ⓂⒶⒸ).

INSERTING IMAGES

1. Place the cursor at the end of the first paragraph, right after the words **all day long.**

2. Press **Enter** (WINDOWS) or **Return** (MAC) to start a new paragraph.

3. In the **Insert** panel, click the **Images** (🖾) button. A menu may drop down, if so choose **Image.**

4. In the dialog that appears, click the **Site Root** button (at the **top** (WINDOWS) or **bottom** (MAC) of the dialog). This ensures you are in the **Dianes Travels** folder.

5. Navigate into the **images** folder and select **san-fran.jpg.**
   Click **OK** (WINDOWS) or **Choose** (MAC).

   NOTE: If you get an **Image Tag Accessibility** dialog, click **change the Accessibility preferences**, uncheck all the options and click **OK.** You can then leave the Image Tag Accessibility dialog blank and click **OK.**

6. Click in the empty space to the right of the image (but still inside the table) and press **Enter** (WINDOWS) or **Return** (MAC) to add an empty line of space below the image.

7. Scroll down to the second paragraph under **Things to Do** and place the cursor before the first word in **Being on Alcatraz.**

8. In the **Insert** panel, click the **Images** (🖾) button.

9. You should already be in the **images** folder, so select **logo-alcatraz.jpg** and click **OK** (WINDOWS) or **Choose** (MAC).

10. We want this image to be beside the text. With the image still selected, in the **Properties** panel, set the **Align** menu to **Left.**

11. Scroll down to the next paragraph and place the cursor before **Fisherman's Wharf.**

12. This time, go to **Insert > Image.**

13. Select **logo-fishmans-wharf.jpg** and click **OK** (WINDOWS) or **Choose** (MAC).

14. With the image still selected, in the **Properties** panel, set the **Align** menu to **Right.**

15. Scroll down to the next paragraph and place the cursor before **For a great outdoor.**

16. Using either **Insert > Image** or the **Images** (🖾) button, insert the image **logo-blazing-saddles.jpg.**

17. With the image still selected, in the **Properties** panel, set **Align** to **Left.**

18. **Save** the file! It would be a shame to lose it all now.

(ADDING A NAVIGATION BAR)

A navigation bar goes in the left column of the table, but that table cell doesn't look wide enough to hold an image. Don't worry. You'll see that things will work out soon enough.

1. Click in the **left** cell of the table. The cursor may be hard to see because it jumps to the vertical center of that tall table cell, but it should be blinking around the top left of the Blazing Saddles image.

2. Use either **Insert > Image** or the **Images** (🖳) button to insert the image **nav-travel-packages.gif.**

3. Notice how the cell width expands to fit the image, although you may have to scroll up or down to see the image. It will be vertically centered in the cell.

4. This navbar really should sit up against the top of the cell, not in the middle. At the bottom of the document's window, in the **Quick Tag Selector,** click the `<tr>` tag to select that table row. It selects both table cells in the row.

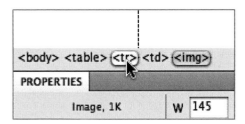

5. In the **Properties** panel, set **Vert** (vertical alignment) to **Top.**

6. Scroll up to the top of the page to find the navbar image, now aligned to the top.

7. Click in the left cell again. The image will probably be selected, and that's fine.

8. Using either **Insert > Image** or the **Images** (🖳) button, insert the image **nav-destination-info.gif.** It will be added after the previous image.

9. Click anywhere in the white space to the left of the table or the text on the right. This should make Dreamweaver refresh the design view preview, which should cause the images to jump onto one line.

10. To fix this click anywhere in the **left** cell.

11. In the **Quick Tag Selector** at the bottom of the window, click the `<td>` tag to select the table cell.

12. In the **Properties** panel, set **W** (width) to **169.** Now the column won't expand, so the images stack vertically on top of each other.

13. Click on the **Destination Info** image.

14. Using either **Insert > Image** or the **Images** ( ) button, insert the rest of the navbar images in this order:
    • **nav-trip-planning.gif**
    • **nav-about.gif**
    • **nav-contact.gif**

15. **Preview** to see it in a browser.

STYLING THE TEXT

Some changes to the text and headings will start to bring the design together.

1. Go into **Modify > Page Properties.**   ⌘J

2. For **Page font,** from the menu (◉) choose **Georgia, Times New Roman, Times, serif.**

3. Below that, for **Size** enter **12** (px).

4. Click **Apply** to preview the changes.

5. On the left side, click the **Headings (CSS)** section.

6. In the **Heading 1** row, enter **20 (px)** and in the color field on the right enter **#6A8E6B.**

7. In the **Heading 2** row, enter **16 (px)** and in the color field enter **#6A8E6B.**

8. Click **OK.**

9. Open the **CSS Styles** panel **(Window > CSS Styles).**

10. At the top of the panel click the **All** button, if it is not selected already.

11. Click the **plus box** (WINDOWS) or **triangle** (MAC) next to **<style>** to display the list of styles. Dreamweaver used CSS for the styling you just did.

12. Since the **Page Properties** dialog we just used for text styling did not offer us an option to change the **Leading** (called **Line Height** in web design) we'll have to edit the style ourselves. In the **CSS Styles** panel double-click the **body,td,th** style.

13. In the dialog that appears set **Line-height** to **17** (px) and click **OK.**
    The lines should now be slightly farther apart.

14. Do a **File > Save** and leave the file open. We'll be using it again in the next exercise.

ID - used for CSS & JavaScript

cmd shift F - opens files window

AH attributes - Remember to add for images.

Adding Link:

Link I ▢ - Browse for a file

DW gives Links borders in Firefox so use Border="0" ✗

External links always use   http://www...

Links to sections w/in page.   "Named Anchor"

coding: <a name ="name" ></a>

Create a TOC

create anchor :   place cursor in destination & select
named Anchor on Common tab & give it a name

select link text : type in link: #name of anchor
↑
Important

code : <a href="name">...
</a>

Back to Top - if using a table, select top left of table & create
a name anchor.

⌘ Y ⇒ Redo (like F4)

Target =_ blank   to open link in a new tab/window

EXERCISE PREVIEW

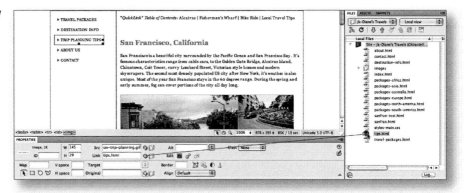

EXERCISE OVERVIEW

Of course Dreamweaver makes it easy to add links to your pages. We'll show you how to link to other pages on your site as well as create link shortcuts within a single page. Also, what if you want to link to an outside website but not have your visitors leave your page? We'll show you how to pop open a new window when they click an outside link.

1. If you completed the previous exercise, **sanfran.html** should still be open and you can skip the following sidebar. If you closed **sanfran.html** re-open it now. We recommend you finish the previous exercise (3A) before starting this one. If you haven't finished it, do the following sidebar.

IF YOU DID NOT DO THE PREVIOUS EXERCISE (3A)

1. In Dreamweaver, go to **Site > Manage Sites.**

2. If you see **yourname-Dianes Travels** select it and click **Remove.** (Click **Yes** to confirm.) This won't remove any files, it just tells Dreamweaver to stop looking at that folder.

3. Click **Done** to close this dialog.

4. Go to **Site > New Site.**

5. A **Site Definition** dialog will open. Click the **Advanced** tab at the top.

6. For **Site name** enter **yourname-Dianes Travels.**

7. Next to **Local root folder**, click on the folder (📁) icon and navigate until you get to **Class Files.** Go into the **yourname-Dreamweaver Class** folder and

   WINDOWS: Double-click on the subfolder **Dianes Travels Ready for Links.** Then click the **Select** button. Click **OK** to finish defining the site.

   MAC: Select the **Dianes Travels Ready for Links** folder and click **Choose.** Click **OK** to finish defining the site.

8. In the **Files** panel double-click **sanfran.html** to open it.

(CREATING LINKS TO PAGES WITHIN YOUR SITE)

1. There are a couple ways to create links. Let's explore them.
    At the top left, select the first navbar image, **Travel Packages.**

2. In the **Properties** panel, next to **Link** click the folder (📁).

3. In the dialog that appears click the **Site Root** button.

4. Choose **travel-packages.html** and click **OK** (WINDOWS) or **Choose** (MAC).

5. Click anywhere in the text on the right to deselect the image.

6. The link brought an unsightly blue border with it. Reselect the **Travel Packages**
    image and in the **Properties** panel, give it a **Border** of **0.**

7. **Preview (F12** (WINDOWS) **or Option–F12** (MAC) **)** the page in a browser and click the
    link to test it.

8. Select the next navbar image, **Destination Info.**

9. In the **Properties** panel, next to **Link** click the folder (📁).

10. Choose **destination-info.html** and click **OK** (WINDOWS) or **Choose** (MAC).

11. With the image still selected, in the **Properties** panel, give it a **Border** of **0.**

12. Let's make another link, but this time we'll see a different way of doing it.
    In the **Files** panel make sure you can see the name of the **tips.html** file.

13. In the page, select the **Trip Planning Tips** navbar image.

14. As shown below, in the **Properties** panel next to **Link,** click and drag the
    Link pointer (⊕) to **tips.html** in the **Files** panel and let go.

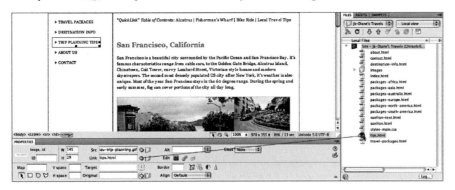

15. With the image still selected, in the **Properties** panel, give it a **Border** of **0.**

16. **Preview (F12** (WINDOWS) **or Option–F12** (MAC) **)** in a web browser and test the links.

17. Let's try that way again, select the **About Us** navbar image.

18. As shown below, from the **Properties** panel, drag the **Link pointer** (⊕) to the **Files** panel, point it at **about.html** and let go.

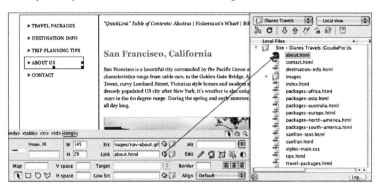

19. Don't forget to give it a **Border** of **0.**

20. Finish up with the final navbar image, **Contact.**

21. Using either the **Browse** (📁) or **Link pointer** (⊕), link it to **contact.html** and set the **Border** to **0.**

CREATING LINKS TO OTHER WEBSITES

1. On the right, under the **Things To Do** heading, select the **Alcatraz Cruises** image.

2. In the **Properties** panel under **Link**, type in: **http://www.alcatrazcruises.com** Then hit **Enter** (WINDOWS) or **Return** (MAC) to apply it.

3. Give it a **Border** of **0.**

4. Preview (**F12** (WINDOWS) or **Option–F12** (MAC)) and test the link (you must have an internet connection to test this link!).

NOTE: If the image didn't become a link it's probably because you typed in the link but didn't hit **Enter** (WINDOWS) or **Return** (MAC) before you previewed. You'll have to repeat the last step and be sure to hit **Enter** (WINDOWS) or **Return** (MAC) to apply the link!

5. A problem with linking to another site is that the user leaves your website — they may forget to come back! The best thing to do is to have the link open in a separate window. That way, the user can visit the other site and then easily return to yours. With the image still selected, in the **Properties** panel next to **Target** click on the menu (⬍) and choose **_blank.**

6. Preview (**F12** (WINDOWS) or **Option–F12** (MAC)) and re-test the link. This time it should open in a new blank window.

7. Let's add another link. Select the **Fisherman's Wharf** image.

8. In the **Properties** panel under **Link**, type in: **http://www.fishermanswharf.org** That's **.org** not .com! Then hit **Enter** (WINDOWS) or **Return** (MAC) to apply it.

9. Give it a **Border** of **0.**

10. Also set the **Target** to **_blank.**

11. Finish up with the last of the three images. Select the **Blazing Saddles** image.

12. Give it a link to **http://www.blazingsaddles.com**
    Don't forget to hit **Enter** (WINDOWS) or **Return** (MAC)!

13. Give it a **Border** of **0.**

14. Once again set **Target** to **_blank.**

15. **Preview** again and test the links.

16. It's been awhile since we last saved changes, go ahead and **Save** now.

LINKS WITHIN A PAGE (NAMED ANCHORS)

In order to make navigating easier, we will insert **named anchors** to sections of the document and then link to those anchors from the Table of Contents. This way a visitor will be able to simply click a link to jump down the page to view a section.

1. For Alcatraz, place the cursor at the start of the paragraph **Being on Alcatraz Island.**

2. Go to **Insert > Named Anchor (Ctrl–Alt–A** (WINDOWS) **or Cmd–Option–A** (MAC)**).**

3. In the dialog box that appears, next to **Anchor name**: type in **alcatraz** and click **OK.**

   NOTE: There cannot be any spaces in anchor names, and it is just easiest to keep everything lower case.

4. You may get a message about not being able to see this element. Check **Don't show me this message again** and click **OK.**

5. Next to the cursor a Dreamweaver invisible element for the **Named Anchor** ( ) may appear. If it does not, go into **View > Visual Aids > Invisible Elements.**

   NOTE: If you still don't see it, that particular invisible element may have been turned off in the preferences. Go into **Edit > Preferences** (WINDOWS) or **Dreamweaver > Preferences** (MAC). On the left side click on **Invisible Elements** and then on the right, check on **Named anchors.**

6. Scroll up to the **"Quicklink" Table of Contents** at the top of the page and highlight **Alcatraz.**

7. In the **Properties** panel press the **HTML** (<> HTML) button to make sure you are editing the HTML properties.

8. In the **Link** field type **#alcatraz** and hit **Enter** (WINDOWS) or **Return** (MAC) to kick it in.

    The # in the link tells the browser to stay on the same page, then the name of the anchor (after the #) says where on the page to scroll to.

9. Test the link by hitting **F12** (WINDOWS) or **Option–F12** (MAC) to preview the page in a web browser. Click on the link. The page should scroll directly down to **Alcatraz.** If it does not, go back to Dreamweaver and make sure the **anchor** and **link** are typed the same and have no spaces.

10. Place the cursor before the first word in the **Fisherman's Wharf** paragraph.

11. In the **Insert** panel, click the **Named Anchor** (🔱) button.

12. In the dialog that appears, next to **Anchor name:** type in **wharf** and click **OK.**

13. Scroll up to the Quicklink Table of Contents at the top of the page and highlight **Fisherman's Wharf.**

14. In the **Properties** panel, in **Link** type **#wharf** and hit **Enter** (WINDOWS) or **Return** (MAC) to kick it in.

15. Let's do one more for **Blazing Saddles.**
    • Insert a **Named Anchor** called **bike**
    • Link the Table of contents **Bike Ride** to **#bike**

16. Hit **F12** (WINDOWS) or **Option–F12** (MAC) and test the links in the web browser. If any of them don't work, check the spelling in the link and anchor.

17. We need a link that brings you back to the top of the page. In the Quick Tag Selector at the bottom of the document, click on the **<body>** tag to select it.

18. Press the **Left Arrow** key to put the cursor at the start of the page. You may not see a blinking cursor, but trust that it's there.

19. In the **Insert** panel, click the **Named Anchor** (🔱) button.

20. Name it **top** and click **OK.**

21. There should now be an anchor icon 🔱 at the top left of the page.

22. Scroll down to the **Alcatraz** paragraph.

23. At the end of the last line in the **Alcatraz** paragraph, select the text **Back to Top.**

24. In the **Properties** panel, give it a link to **#top.**

25. **Preview** with **F12** (WINDOWS) or **Option–F12** (MAC) and give it a try.

26. We want to add the same link to the next two paragraphs. There's a really quick way to do this. In the next paragraph (Fisherman's Wharf), select the text **Back to Top.**

27. Go to **Edit > Redo (Ctrl–Y** (WINDOWS) or **Cmd–Y** (MAC)**).**

28. That's it, the same link has been made again! **Redo** can be used to add the same link, apply the same styling multiple times, and much more. Use it whenever you need to do something over and over again, it's a great timesaver!

29. In the next paragraph, select the text **Back to Top.**

30. Press **Ctrl–Y** (WINDOWS) or **Cmd–Y** (MAC) to **Redo** the link.

31. **Preview** it to make sure the links work.

32. **Save** the file.

CREATING AN EMAIL LINK

1. In the **Files** panel, double-click the file **contact.html** to open it.

2. At the bottom of the page place the cursor in the empty line below **Email.**

3. In the **Insert** panel, click the **Email Link** (🖃) button.

4. Type the following:

   > Text: **diane@dianestravels.com**
   > E-Mail: **diane@dianestravels.com**

   Click **OK.**

5. **Preview (F12** (WINDOWS) or **Option–F12** (MAC)**)** the page and click the email link. If the computer is properly set up it should launch an email program.

   (If your user's email program isn't properly setup, or if they use web based email like Yahoo mail, they'll still know the address by looking at the webpage.)

6. **Save** this file, we're going to continue using it in the next exercise.

7. We are done with this page so you can close the file.

8. You should now be back in the **sanfran.html.** Leave it open since we'll use it in the next exercise.

EXERCISE PREVIEW

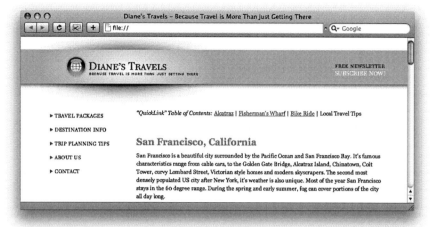

EXERCISE OVERVIEW

You'll continue fleshing out the site by adding a header image to all your pages.
We show you how to do it by adding a background image.

1. If you completed the previous exercise, **sanfran.html** should still be open and
   you can skip the following sidebar. If you closed **sanfran.html** re-open it now.
   We recommend you finish the previous exercises (3A & 3B) before starting this
   one. If you haven't finished them, do the following sidebar.

   IF YOU DID NOT DO THE PREVIOUS EXERCISES (3A & 3B)

   1. In Dreamweaver, go to **Site > Manage Sites.**

   2. If you see **yourname-Dianes Travels** select it and click **Remove.** (Click **Yes** to confirm.)

   3. Click **Done** to close this dialog.

   4. Go to **Site > New Site.**

   5. A **Site Definition** dialog will open. Click the **Advanced** tab at the top.

   6. For **Site name** enter **yourname-Dianes Travels.**

   7. Next to **Local root folder**, click on the folder (📁) icon and navigate until you get to
      Class Files. Go into the **yourname-Dreamweaver Class** folder and

      (WINDOWS): Double-click on the subfolder **Dianes Travels Ready for BG Images.**
      Then click the **Select** button. Click **OK** to finish defining the site.

      (MAC): Select the **Dianes Travels Ready for BG Images** folder and click **Choose.**
      Click **OK** to finish defining the site.

   8. In the **Files** panel double-click **sanfran.html** to open it.

ADDING A HEADER IMAGE

This site could use a header image, but where do we put it? It will need a two column table, but since the column widths are different than our current table, we'll make a new table above the current one.

1. Place the cursor to the right of the **top anchor symbol** (📙).

2. Create a table by clicking the **Table** (▦) button in the **Common** tab of the **Insert** panel or going to **Insert > Table.**

3. Put in these specs:

Rows:	**1**	Columns:	**2**
Table width:	**750 (pixels)**		
Border thickness:	**0**		
Cell padding:	**0**		
Cell spacing:	**0**		
Header:	**None**		

    Leave the Accessibility options as is.
    Click **OK.**

4. With the table still selected, in the **Properties** panel change **Align** to **Center.**

5. Place the cursor in the left cell of the new table.

6. To insert an image, choose **Insert > Image** (or click the **Images** (🖼) button).

7. In the dialog that appears click the **Site Root** button.

8. Go into the **images** folder, and double-click **dianes-travels-logo.jpg.**

9. Click in the right cell of the new table.

10. Using either **Insert > Image** or the **Images** (🖼) button, insert the image **subscribe.gif.**

11. Press the **left arrow** key to move the cursor next to the subscribe image.

12. In the **Properties** panel, set **Horz** (horizontal alignment) to **Right.**

no repeat - appear top left
repeat X - along X axis
Y - " Y axis

BACKGROUND IMAGE

The header images are just floating there in the white, and they don't look great. However, a background image can tie them together and save the design.

1. To add the background, go into **Modify > Page Properties.**

2. Next to **Background image**, click **Browse.**
    In the **images** folder choose **background-header.gif.**

3. Click the **Apply** button to see what it will look like.

4. Yuck! The background image by default will repeat again and again in "rows" and "columns". We want it to repeat only from left to right (like one "row" of images). From the **Repeat** menu ( ) choose **repeat-x.** NOTE: the x axis goes left to right, the y axis goes top to bottom.

5. Click the **Apply** button to see the change. Better, but it still doesn't line up!

6. Under **Margins** set all 4 values (left, right, top and bottom) to **0** (px).

7. Click **Apply** one last time.

8. Closer, but still not there. Click **OK.**

9. Dreamweaver needs a place to put the invisible items, like that anchor symbol ( ). Don't worry, it won't look like this in the browser. **Preview** now to see for yourself.

10. To temporarily hide these invisible items, at the top of the document, click the **Visual Aids** ( ) button and choose **Invisible Elements.**

11. When satisfied, click the **Visual Aids** ( ) button again and choose **Invisible Elements** to show them again.

12. Select the **Diane's Travels logo** at the top left of the header.

13. This should link to the homepage. In the **Properties** panel use either the **Browse** ( ) or **Link pointer** ( ), link it to **index.html.**

    NOTE: A website's first page is called **index.html.**

14. In the **Properties** panel set the **Border** to **0.**

15. Go to **File > Save.**

(ADDING THE HEADER TO OTHER WEBPAGES)

1. Since the header is complete, we can copy and paste it onto other pages. Click anywhere in the header table.

2. At the bottom of the document window, in the Quick Tag Selector click on the `<table>` tag to select the entire table.

3. Go to **Edit > Copy.**

4. In the **Files** panel double-click **contact.html** to open it.

5. Go to **Edit > Paste.**

6. The background image will not have come with the header. To add it, go into **Modify > Page Properties.**

7. Next to **Background image**, click **Browse.** In the **images** folder choose **background-header.gif.**

8. From the **Repeat** menu ( ) choose **repeat-x.**

EXERCISE

9. Click **OK.**

10. Go to **File > Save.**

11. **Close** the file.

12. You should be back in **sanfran.html. Preview** it in a web browser.

13. Click **Contact** in the navbar to see how the site is finally coming together!

14. If you want more practice, you can add the header to the remaining pages in the **Dianes Travel** folder. To review the process:
    • Open a page.
    • Paste in the page header table.
    • Set the background image to **background-header.gif** with **repeat-x.**

EXERCISE PREVIEW

▶ TRAVEL PACKAGES

▶ DESTINATION INFO

▶ TRIP PLANNING TIPS

▶ ABOUT US

▶ CONTACT

EXERCISE OVERVIEW

To create a rollover, or "mouse over" as some people call it, you simply need two images that are the same pixel size (width and height). Dreamweaver can't create the images, but you can create them in Fireworks, Photoshop or whatever image editor you like. Since we've already created the images for your rollovers, using Dreamweaver to create the actual rollover effect won't be hard.

1. If you completed the previous exercise, **sanfran.html** should still be open and you can skip the following sidebar. If you closed **sanfran.html** re-open it now. We recommend you finish the previous exercises (3A–3C) before starting this one. If you haven't finished them, do the following sidebar.

IF YOU DID NOT DO THE PREVIOUS EXERCISES (3A–3C)

1. In Dreamweaver, go to **Site > Manage Sites.**

2. If you see **yourname-Dianes Travels** select it and click **Remove.** (Click **Yes** to confirm.)

3. Click **Done** to close this dialog.

4. Go to **Site > New Site.**

5. A **Site Definition** dialog will open. Click the **Advanced** tab at the top.

6. For **Site name** enter **yourname-Dianes Travels.**

7. Next to **Local root folder**, click on the folder (📁) icon and navigate until you get to **Class Files.** Go into the **yourname-Dreamweaver Class** folder and

    (WINDOWS): Double-click on the subfolder **Dianes Travels Ready for Rollovers.** Then click the **Select** button. Click **OK** to finish defining the site.

    (MAC): Select the **Dianes Travels Ready for Rollovers** folder and click **Choose.** Click **OK** to finish defining the site.

8. In the **Files** panel double-click **sanfran.html** to open it.

Image Rollovers **DREAMWEAVER CS4**

EXERCISE

*Javascript for
dynamic interaction
DW offers Behaviors*

SETTING THINGS UP

1. Before adding a rollover you should name the image. Select the **Travel Packages** button in the navbar on the left.

2. In the **Properties** panel, in the **ID** field, name it **packages** as shown below:

*up image - image when
no rollover

over image - rollover
image*

NAME GOES HERE

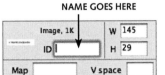

ADDING THE ROLLOVER BEHAVIOR

1. Go to **Window > Behaviors**. This opens the **Behaviors** section of the **Tag Inspector** panel.

2. Click the **Plus** ([+]) button and from the menu that appears select **Swap Image.**

3. At the top of the dialog that appears, the image should already be chosen, so just click the **Browse** button below.

4. In the dialog that opens click the **Site Root** button.

5. Go into the **images** folder and choose **nav-travel-packages_over.gif**.

6. Click **Choose** or **OK** until you close the **Swap Image** dialog.

7. Hit **F12** (WINDOWS) or **Option–F12** (MAC) to preview the page in a browser and roll your mouse over the image. If you are on a **PC** using **Internet Explorer** the rollover may not work. If so read the sidebar below, otherwise continue on to the next step.

ROLLOVERS NOT WORKING IN INTERNET EXPLORER?

When using Internet Explorer in Windows XP Service Pack 2 or later, you may get a yellow bar that prevents rollovers from working. If you upload this page to a webserver it will work, but for security reasons IE prevents the JavaScript from working when previewed locally. To fix that:

- In Dreamweaver go to **Commands > Insert Mark of the Web.**
- Now **Preview** and watch it work! (If it still doesn't work, close all Internet Explorer windows, then preview again.)

ROLLOVERS FOR THE REST OF THE NAVBAR

1. Now you'll repeat this process to add rollovers to the rest of the navbar buttons. Let's review the steps:
   • Select the image.
   • In the **Properties** panel name it appropriately.
   • With the image selected, in In the **Behaviors** section of the **Tag Inspector** panel **(Window > Behaviors)** click the ✚, and select **Swap Image.**
   • Click **Browse** and choose the appropriate images, which are all named the same as the image, but with an **_over** at the end.

2. Add rollovers to the rest of the navbar images using the information below.

IMAGE	ID (NAME)	ROLLOVER IMAGE
Destination Info	info	nav-destination-info_over.gif
Trip Planning Tips	planning	nav-trip-planning_over.gif
About Us	about	nav-about_over.gif
Contact	contact	nav-contact_over.gif

3. Once you've finished, preview in a browser and test out the navbar.

4. Do a **File > Save.**

Disjointed Swaps

rollover X but Y changes

Select hot spot   open Behavior window   and set up swap as before

* 1st Name the image to swap   Be sure to select the image to swap.

Multiple Swaps   on one mouse-over

Select rollover image bring up swap image

double click "Swap image" for "on MouseOver"

EXERCISE PREVIEW

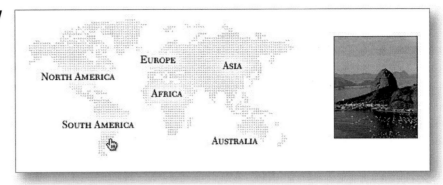

EXERCISE OVERVIEW

In this final installment of the Diane's Travel site we'll add an image map with rollovers. When users roll their mouse over a continent the graphic to the right of the map will change. Dreamweaver makes this easy with its built in Behaviors.

1. If you completed the previous exercises (3A–3D) you should have a Dreamweaver site defined for Diane's Travels so you can skip over the following sidebar. If you haven't finished the previous exercises, do the following sidebar.

IF YOU DID NOT DO THE PREVIOUS EXERCISES (3A–3D)

1. In Dreamweaver, go to **Site > Manage Sites.**

2. If you see **yourname-Dianes Travels** select it and click **Remove.** (Click **Yes** to confirm.)

3. Click **Done** to close this dialog.

4. Go to **Site > New Site.**

5. A **Site Definition** dialog will open. Click the **Advanced** tab at the top.

6. For **Site name** enter **yourname-Dianes Travels.**

7. Next to **Local root folder**, click on the folder (📁) icon and navigate until you get to **Class Files.** Go into the **yourname-Dreamweaver Class** folder and

   (WINDOWS): Double-click on the subfolder **Dianes Travels Ready for Image Maps.** Then click the **Select** button. Click **OK** to finish defining the site.

   (MAC): Select the **Dianes Travels Ready for Image Maps** folder and click **Choose.** Click **OK** to finish defining the site.

---

2. Go to **File > Open.**

3. In the dialog that appears click the **Site Root** button.

4. Double-click **destination-info.html** to open it.

INSERTING THE WORLD MAP

1. Place the cursor in the empty cell to the right of the navbar.

2. In the **Insert** panel click the **Images** (🖼) button.

3. In the dialog that appears click the **Site Root** button.

4. Go into the **images** folder and double-click on **world-map.png**.

DRAWING THE IMAGE MAP

In this graphic we want each continent to have its own link.
That's where image mapping comes in.

1. Select the world map graphic.

2. At the bottom left of the **Properties** panel select the **Rectangular** hotspot tool.

RECTANGULAR HOTSPOT

3. Start with **South America.** Click and drag a rectangle around the continent to draw the hotspot.

4. Next is **North America.** Drag another rectangle around North America, but make sure you don't cross into South America's hotspot.

5. Continue this for **Europe, Africa,** and **Asia.** Do NOT do Australia with a rectangle.

6. Select the **Polygon** hotspot tool.

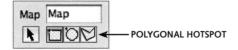
POLYGONAL HOTSPOT

7. Normally with the Polygon hotspot tool you just click to draw a freeform shape. Due to a bug, the Polygon tool sometimes doesn't draw shapes, it just makes points without connecting them. The fix is to hold **Shift** while you click. Don't ask us why it works, it just does. Holding **Shift**, click to place points that follow the edges of Australia. Leave some space around it, and don't forget the word Australia too!

8. Choose the **Pointer Hotspot** (🔺) tool (to the far left of the **Polygon** hotspot tool) and click on the image outside of your shape. This closes the hotspot.

9. When finished, it should look something like this:

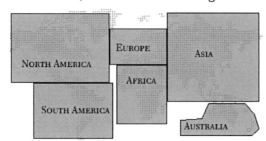

ADDING THE LINKS

We've already created the individual pages for each continent, so all you have to do is create links from the hotspots to the page in the site.

1. Click on the **South America** hotspot to select it.

2. In the **Properties** panel next to **Link,** click the **browse** folder (🗀).

3. In the dialog that appears click the **Site Root** button.

4. Double-click **packages-south-america.html** to choose it.

5. Hit **F12** ⟨WINDOWS⟩ or **Option–F12** ⟨MAC⟩ to preview in a browser.

6. Click **South America.** You should be taken to the South America destination page.

7. Let's do another one to make sure we have the hang of this. In Dreamweaver, select the **North America** hotspot.

8. In the **Properties** panel next to **Link,** click the **browse** folder (🗀) and choose **packages-north-america.html.**

   ⟨WINDOWS⟩ **Only (Windows XP Service Pack 2 and later):** If testing your links in Internet Explorer, go to **Commands > Remove Mark of the Web.** For some reason this prevents image maps from working properly.

9. **Preview** and test out the links.

10. You don't have to do them all, but if you have time do a few more to make sure you get it, go ahead. Otherwise continue on.

ADDING ROLLOVERS

We are going to assign rollover behaviors to each of these hotspots, but we are not going to change the world map graphic. We are going to add an image to the right of the map and have it display a preview of the continent while we rollover the map.

1. Click to the right of the world map so the cursor is blinking next to it.

2. Using either **Insert > Image** or the **Images** (🖼) button, insert the image **preview-tour-pricing.gif.**

3. With the image still selected, at the top left of the **Properties** panel, in the **ID** field, name it **preview** (we must name it so when we add the rollover behavior we'll be able to identify it from the other images).

4. Select the **South America** hotspot.

5. In the **Behaviors** section of the **Tag Inspector** panel **(Window > Behaviors)** click the ⊞ and select **Swap Image.**

6. As shown below, in the **Swap Image** dialog box that appears, all the images on the page are listed in the Images field. Dreamweaver assumes you want to swap the map (which we didn't name), but we don't. We want to swap the **preview** image. Select **image "preview"** and then click **Browse.**

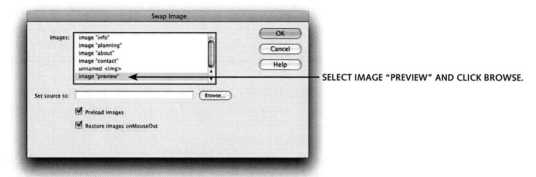

SELECT IMAGE "PREVIEW" AND CLICK BROWSE.

7. In the dialog that appears click the **Site Root** button.

8. Go into the **images** folder and double-click **preview-south-america.jpg.**

9. Leave both **Preload images** and **Restore images onMouseOut** checked. Click **OK.**

10. **Preview.** Test out the rollover behavior to make sure everything works. If testing in **Internet Explorer on the PC** a yellow bar will appear at the top of the page. You must click on the yellow bar and choose **Allow Blocked Content** and then click **Yes.** Then you can test out the page normally.

11. Select the **North America** hotspot.

12. In the **Behaviors** section of the **Tag Inspector** panel **(Window > Behaviors)** click the ⊞ and select **Swap Image.**

13. Select the **image "preview"** and click **Browse.**

14. In the **images** folder double-click **preview-north-america.jpg.**

15. Leave both **Preload images** and **Restore images onMouseOut** checked. Click **OK.**

16. **Preview** again to make sure it's working as well.

(MORE PRACTICE)

If you feel like you understand everything you don't have to finish doing the rollovers for the rest of the continents, but keep going if you want to finish up the whole page.

1. Follow the instructions below if you need a reminder for doing the rollover.
   • Select a hotspot.
   • In the Behaviors section of the Tag Inspector panel click the ⊞ and select Swap Image.
   • Select **image "preview"** and click **Browse.**

- Refer to the chart for the rollover images.

Hotspot:	Set Swap Image to:
Europe	preview-europe.gif
Africa	preview-africa.gif
Asia	preview-asia.gif
Australia	preview-australia.gif

2. **Save** and **Preview** the file!

3. **Close** all files that you have open. We're done with Diane's Travels.

CASCADING STYLE SHEETS

Styling Text and Links using CSS

Different Types of Styles and When to Use Each Type:

    Custom Styles (Class Selectors)

    Redefining HTML Tags

    Advanced Selectors (for Link Styles)

External Style Sheets (Site-Wide Styles)

LAYERS (AP DIVS)

Using Absolute Positioned Layers to Lay Out a Page

SITE MANAGEMENT (SITEWIDE LAYOUT & CONTENT CHANGES)

Templates

Libraries

Divs ⇒ Layers

    Layout Tab → AP Div   (Absolutely Positioned)
                           w/ Left ∘ Top Coordinates

External Style Sheets.

    CSS Styles (window)

        Can Duplicate styles & then modify

Link Styles   a. link   ← Apply styles in
                    a. visted   this order !!
    Compound   a. hover
                    a. active

STYLE PRECEDENTS

External Style Sheet

    Internal styles overwrite external styles

      Inline styles overwrite Internal styles

Elements can have names - apply a style by naming it
!Must be named in Properties box!   #, name,

CSS-P Element Properties
        Dimensions : must type "PX" or "%"
          H : type auto to autofit to content.

                            box
Gaps around edge of content · CSS Styles   set margin to 0

Nav Bars → wrapping   css style set CSS-P elements
                         Block → No Wrap

EXERCISE PREVIEW

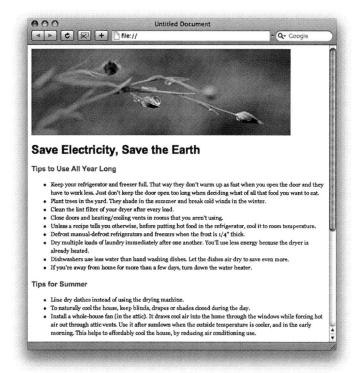

EXERCISE OVERVIEW

This is the first in a series of exercises that shows you some more advanced layout techniques. We will start by adding some CSS styles and sharing them between the pages of a site.

DEFINING A SITE

We're going to be working with a new site about solar energy. We have prepared a folder of images and partially made webpages for you to finish. Let's define a site in Dreamweaver to tell it about this new website folder.

1. In Dreamweaver, go to **Site > New Site.**

2. A **Site Definition** dialog will open. If not already showing, click the **Advanced** tab at the top of the dialog.

3. For **Site name** enter **yourname-NY Solar.**

4. Next to **Local root folder**, click on the folder ( ) icon and navigate until you get to **Class Files.** Go into the **yourname-Dreamweaver Class** folder and

   (**WINDOWS**): Double-click on the subfolder **NY Solar.**
   Click the **Select** button, then click **OK** to finish defining the site.

   (**MAC**): Select the **NY Solar** folder and click **Choose.**
   Click **OK** to finish defining the site.

CASCADING STYLE SHEETS (CSS)

CSS can be a huge time saver and a way to ensure that the site maintains a consistent look. Once set up, you can change a site's font, size, or style simply by editing the styles, rather than each individual page. All current browsers support CSS very well. They may not render the more advanced CSS features exactly the same way, but that should not be an issue for the CSS we use in this workbook.

1. Go to the **Files** panel **(Window > Files)** and double-click **tips.html.**
   The text has already been assigned appropriate headings and is ready for styling.

2. Open the **CSS Styles** panel **(Window > CSS Styles).**

3. As shown below, click the **New CSS Rule** ( ) button at the bottom right.

4. In the dialog that appears (don't click OK until we tell you to):
   • At the top set **Selector Type** to **Tag.**
   • In the middle, under **Selector Name,** type in **li** (You are typing this because **li** is the tag for list item, therefore this style will affect all the bulleted lists!).
   • At the bottom under **Rule Definition** choose **(New Style Sheet File).**
   This makes a separate CSS file and links the current HTML file to it, allowing the styles to be used across numerous webpages. The **Rule Definition** tells Dreamweaver where to put the CSS Rule.

5. Click **OK.**

6. You will be asked to save the CSS file:
   • Click the **Site Root** button.
   • Name it **styles-main.css** and click **Save.**

7. After clicking **Save** you'll be in the **CSS Rule Definition** dialog.
   Set the following:
   Font-family: **Georgia, Times New Roman, Times, serif**
   Font-size: **12** (px)
   Line-height: **17** (px)

8. Click **OK.**

9. Click anywhere in the top Heading 1, **Save Electricity, Save the Earth.**

10. In the **CSS Styles panel,** click the **New CSS Rule** ( ) button.

CSS STYLES BUG AND DW CS3

Although it has been fixed in version CS4, **Mac OS 10.5 (Leopard)** had some bugs with Dreamweaver CS3. Sometimes Dreamweaver would add an additional **.css** to the style sheet link or to the file itself. If using CS3, the way to avoid having your style sheet disappear, is to **NOT** type the **.css** at the end of the name while saving the style sheet. If your styles do get lost, check both the style sheet file name in the finder and in the link in the code.

11. In the dialog that appears:
    - At the top set the **Selector Type** to **Tag.**
    - In the middle under **Selector Name,** notice that it automatically says **h1.** Dreamweaver knew you wanted to redefine the h1 tag because the cursor was inside an h1 tag!
    - At the bottom under **Rule Definition,** make sure **styles-main.css** is chosen.

12. Click **OK.**

13. Set the following:
    Font-family: **Arial, Helvetica, sans-serif.**
    Font-size: **24 (px)**

14. Click **OK.**

15. Click anywhere in the second line, the Heading 2, **Tips to Use All Year Long.**

16. In the **CSS Styles** panel, click the **New CSS Rule** ( ) button.

17. Set the **Selector Type** to **Tag,** make sure the **Selector Name** says **h2,** and check that the **Rule Definition** is set to **styles-main.css.**

    Then click **OK.**

18. Set the following:
    Font-family: **Arial, Helvetica, sans-serif.**
    Font-size: **15 (px)**
    Color: **#367031**

19. Click **OK.**

20. In the **CSS Styles** panel, click the **plus** (WINDOWS) or **triangle** (MAC) next to **styles-main.css** to view the styles inside.

21. Click on the individual rules to see the properties of each one in the bottom half of the **CSS Styles** panel. If you don't see this section you may have to make the panel taller, or drag the **Properties** divider up higher.

22. Select the **li** rule.

23. At the top right corner of the **CSS Styles** panel, go into the **Panel Menu** ( ) and choose **Duplicate.**

24. In the **Selector Name** section, type **p** and click **OK.**
    Wow, that was quick! Now the **paragraphs** (like the one at the bottom of the page) are styled the same as the list items.

25. Place the cursor at the beginning of the page, before the first word **Save.**

26. Go to **Insert > Image.**

27. In the dialog that appears click the **Site Root** button.

28. Go into the **images** folder and double-click **banner-go-green.jpg.**

29. Press the **right arrow** once to move the cursor next to the image.

30. Press **Enter** (WINDOWS) or **Return** (MAC).

31. Press the **left arrow** once to move the cursor back next to the image.

32. Notice that the image inherited the h1 tag from the header below. Let's fix it.

33. In the **Properties** panel, press the **HTML** (<> HTML) button to make sure you are editing the HTML properties.

34. To get rid of the h1 tag, change the Format from **Heading 1** to **none.**

CREATING AND APPLYING CUSTOM (CLASS) STYLES

Redefining tags is great, but sometimes you need to style something that doesn't have a specific tag. That's when you need a custom (class) style.

1. In the **CSS Styles** panel click **New CSS Rule** ( ).

2. Don't click OK until we say!
   • Set the **Selector Type** to **Class.**
   • In the under **Selector Name**, type in **solar-fact**
   • Under **Rule Definition** leave **styles-main.css** chosen.

3. Click **OK.**

4. In the **CSS Rule Definition** dialog set the following:
   Font-family: **Verdana, Geneva, sans-serif.**
   Font-size: **10 (px)**
   Line-height: **18 (px)**

5. Click **OK.**

6. Now you must apply this style. Scroll down to the bottom of the document and click anywhere in the **Solar Fact of the Day** bold text.

7. In the Quick Tag Selector at the bottom of the window, click on the **<p>** tag to select the title and the text below it.

8. In the **Properties** panel be sure you are editing the **HTML** (<> HTML) properties.

9. From the **Class** menu choose **solar-fact.**

10. Go to **File > Save All** and **Preview** the page in a browser.

SHARING STYLE SHEETS

1. In the **Files** panel, double-click the file **contact.html.**

2. This page does not yet use the styles you created on the previous page. In the **CSS Styles** panel click the **Attach Style Sheet** ( ) button near the bottom right.

3. Click the **Browse** button.

4. In the dialog that appears click the **Site Root** button.

5. Choose **styles-main.css.**

6. Hit **Choose** and/or **OK** until you are out of all the dialogs. Now you should see that the headings and paragraphs look like the other page.

7. At the bottom of the document, click anywhere in the **Enviro-Mail** title.

8. In the Quick Tag Selector at the bottom of the window, click on the **<p>** tag to select the title and the text below it.

9. In the **Properties** panel make sure you are in the HTML (<> HTML) section and from the **Class** menu choose **solar-fact.**
   See, all the styles are there for you to use!

CHANGING STYLES AFTER THEY HAVE BEEN USED

1. Let's say we don't like the green color we chose for the Heading 2's. Go to the **CSS Styles** panel.

2. Expand the **styles-main.css** stylesheet so you can see the styles inside.

3. Click once on the **h2** style to select it.

4. You should see the Properties for the style displayed below. If not, you may need to resize the panel to see them (so it looks like the screenshot on the right).

5. As shown to the right, click on the color. Then type in **#1A619A.**

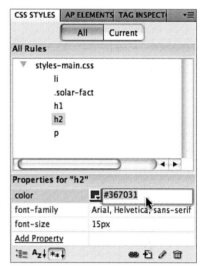

6. Switch to the **tips.html** file. Notice both files have now changed from green to blue.

7. Switch back to **contact.html.**

STYLING THE LINKS

Text links by default have a blue color and an underline. Let's customize that look.

1. In the **CSS Styles** panel, click **New CSS Rule** (🔳) and:
   • set the **Selector Type** to **Compound**
   • in the middle under **Selector Name** click on the menu (🔹) and choose **a:link**
   • under **Rule Definition** leave **styles-main.css** chosen

   Click **OK.**

2. Under **Color,** type in **#1A619A** and click **OK.**

3. Let's add some pizzazz with a style for when the mouse is hovering over the link. In the **CSS Styles** panel click **New CSS Rule** (🔳) and:
   • set the **Selector Type** to **Compound**
   • in the middle under to **Selector Name** click on the menu (🔹) and choose **a:hover**
   • under **Rule Definition** leave **styles-main.css** chosen

4. Click **OK.**

5. Under **Text-decoration**, check **none.**

6. Click **OK.**

7. Go to **File > Save All.**

8. **Preview** in a browser and be sure to mouse over the link to see the effect.

ORGANIZING STYLES

1. The styles are in somewhat of a random order. Let's put them into a better order. This will make future updates easier. Make sure the **CSS Styles** panel is tall enough to see all the styles.

2. Drag the **.solar-fact** style to the bottom of the list.

3. Drag the **p** style above the **a:link** style.

4. Drag the **li** style above the **a:link** style (which means the **li** style will now be below the **p** style).

5. As shown to the right, the more general tag redefine styles are now listed first, then the more specific class style is at the end.

6. Go to **File > Save All.**
   Leave the files open because you'll use them in the next exercise.

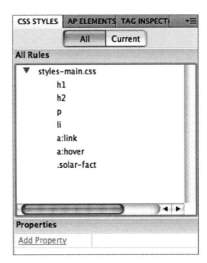

NOTE: Be sure to upload the .css file to the web server when you upload all the files, because the pages are linked to it!

CSS LINK STYLING ORDER	CSS TYPE SIZE
The order of link styles in the code matters! If they are written out of order they may not work properly. The correct order should always be: 1. a:link 2. a:visited 3. a:hover 4. a:active	Even though you "can" choose **points** for font size, it is best to use **pixels** to make sure fonts will display exactly the same size in different browsers on various platforms (Windows, Mac, etc.). **Pixels** are a screen measurement while **points** are a print measurement. While web browsers often translate points into pixels the same way, using points could potentially yield different sizes on various platforms. Using **pixels** ensures that text will be the same size on all platforms because it is the correct type of measurement for the media (the screen).

EXERCISE PREVIEW

EXERCISE OVERVIEW

Layers are a great layout tool that offer more design flexibility than tables. You'll create the header and sidebar on this page to give you a handle on how to use them.

Layers (which Dreamweaver calls AP Divs) are another way of laying out a page. Earlier we used tables for the same purpose. Layers offer more flexibility and options than tables.

1. Before we get started, let's set a preference that prevents layers from being unintentionally tied together. Go to **Edit > Preferences** (WINDOWS) or **Dreamweaver > Preferences** (MAC).

2. On the left click on **AP Elements.**

3. On the right uncheck the checkbox next to **Nesting.**

4. Click **OK.**

5. If you completed the previous exercise, **tips.html** should be open and you can skip the following sidebar. If you closed **tips.html** re-open it now. We recommend you finish the previous exercise (4A) before starting this one. If you haven't finished it, do the following sidebar.

IF YOU DID NOT DO THE PREVIOUS EXERCISE (4A)

1. In Dreamweaver, go to **Site > Manage Sites.**

2. If you see **yourname-NY Solar** select it and click **Remove.** (Click **Yes** to confirm.)

3. Click **Done** to close this dialog.

4. Go to **Site > New Site.**

5. A **Site Definition** dialog will open. Click the **Advanced** tab at the top.

6. For **Site name** enter **yourname-NY Solar.**

7. Next to **Local root folder,** click on the folder (📁) icon and navigate until you get to **Class Files.** Go into the **yourname-Dreamweaver Class** folder and

   WINDOWS: Double-click on the subfolder **NY Solar Ready for Layers.**
   Then click the **Select** button. Click **OK** to finish defining the site.

   MAC: Select the **NY Solar Ready for Layers** folder and click **Choose.**
   Click **OK** to finish defining the site.

8. In the **Files** panel double-click **tips.html** to open it.

---

6. In **tips.html** select all the content on the page **(Edit > Select All).**

7. **Cut** it.

8. In the **Insert** panel, click the **Layout** tab.

9. Click the **Draw AP Div** (📰) button.
   You may not see the button change, but the cursor will be a crosshair when over the document.

10. **Click and drag** out a layer on the left side that covers around half of the document. We'll fine tune the size and position later.

11. Click inside the layer so that it's highlighted blue and there is a large blinking cursor (which will be a bit hard to see, but it's there).

12. **Paste** the text/picture.

13. The layer should have a selection handle (🔲) at the top left. If not, click anywhere in the layer and the handle should appear.

14. Click on the layer selection handle (🔲) to select the layer and display its options in the **Properties** panel.

15. Notice at the top left of the **Properties** panel that the layer is named **apDiv1.**

16. In the **CSS Styles** panel, click the **plus box** **WINDOWS** or **triangle** **MAC** to expand **<style>** and see the list of styles.

17. The **#apDiv1** style gives the layer its position and size. The **#** means the style targets something by a name, which is why the style is named the same as the layer. Go back to the **Properties** panel and change the name from **apDiv1** to **main-content.**

18. Notice that the name of the style has also changed in the **CSS Styles** panel!

19. In the **Properties** panel let's set the position. Set **L** (left) to **26px** and a **T** (top) to **134px.** These tell the browser how far from the left and top of the window to position the layer.

20. Look in the **CSS Styles** panel at the **#main-content** style. This is the style that positions the **main-content** layer. Select it so you can see the **left** and **top** numbers that we just set (they appear in the bottom section of the panel).

21. Now lets match the layer's width to the width of the image. Make sure the **main-content** layer is still selected. If not, click anywhere inside the layer, then click on the layer selection handle (⊞).

22. In the **Properties** panel, give it a **W** (width) of **548px** and for **H** (height) type **auto.** Auto height means that the layer will automatically size itself to fit the content.

(MAKING A SIDEBAR)

1. At the bottom of the text, click anywhere in the **Solar Fact of the Day** text.

2. In the Quick Tag Selector at the bottom of the window click on the **<p.solar-fact>** tag to select the paragraph.

3. **Cut** the text.

4. In the **Insert** panel, click the **Draw AP Div** (⊞) button.

5. **Click and drag** out a layer to the right of the **main-content** layer.

6. Click inside the layer.

7. **Paste** the text.

8. Click on this new layer's layer handle (⊞) to select it.

9. In the **Properties** panel, name this layer **sidebar.**

10. Also in the **Properties** panel set the following settings:

      L: **602px**   W: **162px**
      T: **134px**   H: **auto**

11. Also in the **Properties** panel, set the **Bg color** to **#666666.**
This will make the text a bit hard to read, but we'll fix that soon.

12. Place the cursor at the beginning of the first line in the sidebar.

13. Press **Enter** (WINDOWS) or **Return** (MAC).

14. Press the **Up Arrow** key to move the cursor into the empty line above the text.

15. Choose **Insert > Image.**

16. Click the **Site Root** button.

17. Go into the **images** folder and double-click **sidebar-top.jpg** to choose it.

18. We don't want the extra space from the paragraph and solar-fact class that the image inherited. Click on the image to select it.

19. In the Quick Tag Selector, **Right-Click** (WINDOWS) or **Control-Click** (MAC) the **<p.solar-fact>** tag and choose **Remove Tag.**

20. Place the cursor at the end of the sidebar.

21. Press **Enter** (WINDOWS) or **Return** (MAC).

22. **Insert** the image **sidebar-bottom.gif.**

23. Again in the Quick Tag Selector, **Right-Click** (WINDOWS) or **Control-Click** (MAC) the **<p.solar-fact>** tag and choose **Remove Tag** to remove the space around this image.

24. Now lets give that text a little padding and make it stand out. In the **CSS Styles** panel, double-click the **solar-fact** style.

25. For color, type **#BBBBBB.**

26. On the left side of the dialog, click the **Box** section.

27. Under Padding, **uncheck Same for All** and type in the following:

> Top: **0**
> Right: **10**
> Bottom: **0**
> Left: **14**

28. Click **OK.**

(HEADER & NAVIGATION BAR)

1. In the **Insert** panel, click the **Draw AP Div** (🖾) button.

2. **Click and drag** out a layer above the other layers.

3. Click inside the layer and **Insert** the image **headerlogo-nysolar.jpg.**

4. Click on this new layer's layer handle (🖽) to select it.

5. In the **Properties** panel, name the layer **header.**

6. Also in the **Properties** panel set the following:

    L: **0px**   W: **100%**
    T: **0px**   H: **auto**

7. Click inside the layer to the right of the logo image.

8. Press **Shift–Enter** (WINDOWS) or **Shift–Return** (MAC) to add a line break.
    You won't notice a new line added yet, but it's there.

9. Insert the following images in this order (they'll form a horizontal navbar):
    • **nav-about.png**
    • **nav-solar.png**
    • **nav-tips.png**
    • **nav-contact.png**

10. In the **CSS Styles** panel, double-click the **#header** style to edit it.

11. On the left side, click the **Background** section.

12. Next to **Background-image,** click **Browse** and from the **images** folder, choose **header-background.jpg.**

13. Below that setting, for **Background-repeat** choose **repeat-x.**

14. Click **OK.**
    The background image now forms a seamless continuation of the logo and nav images.

15. **Preview** in a browser to see your work so far. Resize the browser window to make it very small. Notice that the top navbar breaks onto multiple lines as the window gets too small. That needs to be fixed.

16. In the **CSS Styles** panel, double-click the **#header** style to edit it again.

17. On the left side, click the **Block** section.

18. Under **White-space,** choose **nowrap.**

19. Click **OK.**

20. **Preview** again and resize the window. Silky smooth.

21. The last thing the page needs is a title. At the top of the document window next to title enter **NY Solar - Tips to Go Green.**

22. Go to **File > Save All.**
    Leave the files open. You'll continue using them in the next exercise.

BONUS PRACTICE IF YOU HAVE EXTRA TIME

You can finish the navbar by adding rollover graphics. The chart below will tell
you the information needed. Remember that to create rollovers you need to name
the image, then go to the **Behaviors** section of the **Tag Inspector** panel and add
the **Swap Image** behavior.

IMAGE	NAME	ROLLOVER IMAGE
About Us	navabout	nav-about_over.gif
Solar For Work & Home	navsolar	nav-solar_over.gif
Tips To Go Green	navtips	nav-tips_over.gif
Contact Us	navcontact	nav-contact_over.gif

[Handwritten notes:]

4C

'padding in a box applied may make box bigger!

Templates & Libraries. (Dreamweaver Specific)

Save As Template —— creates a Template subfolder
    └ Update Links? - Yes
        templates are locked up.

To make editable, select div   Insert > Temp Objects > Editable Region
                                    & name regions. → Save
                                Now can open new page from Template

☑ update page when Template is Δ'd

Apply Templates to a Page - Modify > Templates > Apply Temp. to Pg

EXERCISE PREVIEW

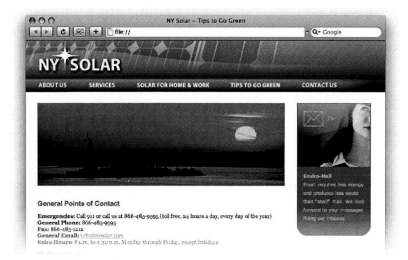

EXERCISE OVERVIEW

In the previous exercises we've done a lot of work to make one header/navbar. We don't want to have to do it again on every single page. That's where templates come in. Templates are best used for creating pages that have many shared elements that will always be exactly the same. We'll quickly create this page using elements we already made from the previous exercise.

CREATING A TEMPLATE

1. Go to **File > Close All.**

2. Dreamweaver's template feature requires a site to be defined. If you completed the previous exercises (4A & 4B) you should have a site defined for **NY Solar** so you can skip over the following sidebar. If you haven't finished the previous exercises (and therefore do not have a **NY Solar** site) do the following sidebar.

IF YOU DID NOT DO THE PREVIOUS EXERCISES (4A & 4B)

1. In Dreamweaver, go to **Site > Manage Sites.**

2. If you see **yourname-NY Solar** select it and click **Remove.** (Click **Yes** to confirm.)

3. Click **Done** to close this dialog.

4. Go to **Site > New Site.**

5. A **Site Definition** dialog will open. Click the **Advanced** tab at the top.

6. For **Site name** enter **yourname-NY Solar.**

7. Next to **Local root folder**, click on the folder (📁) icon and navigate until you get to **Class Files.** Go into the **yourname-Dreamweaver Class** folder and

   WINDOWS: Double-click on the subfolder **NY Solar Ready for Templates.** Then click the **Select** button. Click **OK** to finish defining the site.

   MAC: Select the **NY Solar Ready for Templates** folder and click **Choose.** Click **OK** to finish defining the site.

---

3. In the **Files** panel, double-click **tips.html** to open it.

4. Go to **File > Save as Template.**

5. Name it **main page** and click **Save.**

6. When Dreamweaver asks you about updating links, click **Yes.**

7. Click anywhere inside the **main-content** layer on the left.

8. **Select All** by pressing **Ctrl–A** (WINDOWS) or **Cmd–A** (MAC).

9. Go into **Insert > Template Objects > Editable Region.**

10. Name it **main** and click **OK.**

11. Click anywhere inside the **sidebar** layer on the right.

12. **Select All** by pressing **Ctrl–A** (WINDOWS) or **Cmd–A** (MAC).

13. Go into **Insert > Template Objects > Editable Region.**

14. Name it **sidebar** and click **OK.**

15. Go to **File > Save.**

16. **Close** the file.

(USING THE TEMPLATE)

1. Now we can create pages from the template we just made. Go to **File > New.**

2. On the left select **Page from Template.**

3. Make sure that **yourname-NY Solar** is the site highlighted and then select **main page**. You should see a preview of the page to the right.

4. Click **Create.**

5. Go to **File > Save As.**

6. Click the **Site Root** button.

7. Name it **tips.html,** replacing the one already there.
   Even though this page was already done, we need to save over the original with this file that uses the template (so it will update later when the template is updated).

8. Look at the right side of the header area to notice that the background image is now missing and the white of the page shows instead. What happened? This is a template glitch that we must fix.

9. Go to the **Assets** panel **(Window > Assets).**

10. On the left click on the **Templates** ( ) section.

11. If you don't see the **main page** template listed, at the bottom right of the panel click the **Refresh Site List** (⟳) button.

12. Click once on the **main page** template to select it.

13. At the top right of the **Assets** panel, go into the **panel menu** (▾≣) and choose **Update Current Page.** We aren't sure why this bug occurs, but at least it is an easy fix.

14. Go to **File > Save.**

> ### MAKING ANOTHER PAGE FROM THE TEMPLATE

1. In the **Files** panel double-click **contact.html** to open it.

2. This content needs to be put into our template. Luckily we can apply templates to existing pages. Go to **Modify > Templates > Apply Template to Page.**

3. In the list of templates click on **main page** and click **Select.**

4. Another dialog will appear:
   • Select **Document body.**
   • Near the bottom of the window, set **Move content to new region** to **main.**
   • Select **Document head** (this is the link to the css file).
   • Near the bottom of the window, set **Move content to new region** to **Nowhere.** (We don't need to keep the link to the CSS file since that is already in the template.)
   • Click **OK.**

5. At the bottom of the page click anywhere in the **Enviro-Mail** text.

6. In the Quick Tag Selector at the bottom of the window, click on the **<p.solar-fact>** tag to select it and the text below.

7. **Cut** the text.

8. In the sidebar on the right of the page, click anywhere in the **Solar Fact** text.

9. In the Quick Tag Selector at the bottom of the window, click on the **<p.solar-fact>** tag to select it and the text below.

10. **Paste** the Enviro-Mail text over that.

11. Let's replace the image at the top of the sidebar.
    Double-click the solar eclipse image above the text.

12. Find **sidebar-top-contact.jpg** and click **OK** (WINDOWS) or **Choose** (MAC).
    Awesome! Double-clicking an image is a quick way to replace it with another.

13. **Preview** in a browser.

14. Go to **File > Save All.**

15. Do a **File > Close All.**

EDITING THE TEMPLATE

Changes made to a template will update all the pages that are based on that template. This makes sitewide content changes faster and easier.

1. Go to the **Assets** panel **(Window > Assets).**
   - On the left click on the **Templates** (📄) section
   - On the right double-click **main page**

2. Select the **about us** image in the navbar.

3. **Insert** the image **nav-services.png.**

4. Go to **File > Save.**

5. You should now see an **Update Template Files** dialog. Hit **Update.**

6. An **Update Pages** dialog will open. If it's not already checked, check **Show Log.** This is a report telling you how many files were updated. Click **Close.**

7. Also close the file.

8. Return to the **Files** panel **(Window > Files).**

9. Open **tips.html,** which is based on the template, to see that it has been updated with the new **services** button.

10. Open **contact.html,** to see that it has also been updated with the new **services** button.

11. Back when we applied the template, the title changed to match the template. At the top of document window, change the title to **NY Solar - Contact Info.**

12. Leave the files open. You'll use them in the next exercise.

OPTIONAL BONUS, IF YOU HAVE EXTRA TIME

You now have the tools to build this entire site. Here's an overview of how:
   - Open a page that doesn't have the template applied, such as:
     about.html, contest.html, home-work.html or **services.html**
   - Go to **Modify > Templates > Apply Template to Page.**
   - In the list of templates click on **main page** and click **Select.**
   - In the next dialog select **Document body** and set **Move content to new region** to **main.** Then click **OK.**
   - Apply the **solar-fact** style to the bottom paragraph (with its bold header) and cut and paste in into the sidebar.
   - At the top of the document window, give the page a unique **Title.** (This text appears in Google or when someone bookmarks the page.)

If you didn't already, you can add rollovers to the nav images and link them to the appropriate pages. Do that on the **main page** template. When you save those changes, Dreamweaver will update all the pages based on that template.

EXERCISE PREVIEW

Win a Free solar panel system in Celbration of our 20 Year Anniversary! ENTER NOW!

EXERCISE OVERVIEW

Libraries let you reuse content across multiple pages. Unlike templates which are an entire page, library items are smaller sections of content and can be used in various places across different pages. Like templates, future edits will update all the pages that use a library item.

1. Dreamweaver's library feature requires a site to be defined. If you completed the previous exercises (4A–4C) you should have a site defined for **NY Solar** so you can skip over the following sidebar. If you haven't finished the previous exercises (and therefore do not have a **NY Solar** site) do the following sidebar.

IF YOU DID NOT DO THE PREVIOUS EXERCISES (4A–4C)

1. In Dreamweaver, go to **Site > Manage Sites.**

2. If you see **yourname-NY Solar** select it and click **Remove.** (Click **Yes** to confirm.)

3. Click **Done** to close this dialog.

4. Go to **Site > New Site.**

5. A **Site Definition** dialog will open. Click the **Advanced** tab at the top.

6. For **Site name** enter **yourname-NY Solar.**

7. Next to **Local root folder**, click on the folder (📁) icon and navigate until you get to **Class Files.** Go into the **yourname-Dreamweaver Class** folder and

8. (WINDOWS): Double-click on the subfolder **NY Solar Ready for Libraries.** Then click the **Select** button. Click **OK** to finish defining the site.

9. (MAC): Select the **NY Solar Ready for Libraries** folder and click **Choose.** Click **OK** to finish defining the site.

(CREATING AND USING LIBRARY ITEMS)

1. If **contact.html** isn't open, go to the **Files** panel and double-click **contact.html.**

2. Click at the bottom of the page, either under the resellers email or to the right of it, so you get a blinking cursor at the end.

3. Hit **Enter** (WINDOWS) or **Return** (MAC) twice to give us some space.

4. Type **Win a Free solar panel system in Celebration of our 19 Year Anniversary!**

4D

EXERCISE

5. In the **CSS Styles** panel click **New CSS Rule** ( ) and specify the following:
   • Set **Selector Type** to **Class.**
   • In the middle next to **Selector Name** type **contest.**
   • Under **Rule Definition** make sure **styles-main.css** is chosen.

   Click **OK.**

6. Set the following:

   Font-family: **Arial, Helvetica, sans-serif**
   Font-size: **12 (px)**
   Font-weight: **bold**

   Click **OK.**

7. Select the line you just typed.

8. In the **Properties** panel be sure you are editing the **HTML** (<> HTML) properties.

9. From the **Class** menu choose **contest.**

10. Press the **right arrow** once to move the cursor to the end of the text and press the **spacebar** once.

11. Go to **Insert > Image.**

12. Click the **Site Root** button.

13. Go into the **images** folder and double-click on **enter-now.png.**

14. With the image still selected, in the **Properties** panel:
    • Set the Border to **0.**
    • From the **Align** menu choose **Absolute Middle.**
    • Next to **Link** click the browse for file ( ) icon.
    • In the dialog that appears click the **Site Root** button.
    • Double-click on **contest.html.**

15. **Preview** in a browser to test the link and make sure everything looks good.

16. Go to the **Assets** panel **(Window > Assets).**

17. On the left side, click the **Library** items ( ) button to show the site's Library items.

18. When selecting the contest line we must be sure to also select the enclosing <p> tags. Click anywhere in the contest text and in the **Quick Tag Selector** at the bottom of the window, click the **<p.contest>** tag.

19. At the bottom of the **Assets** panel click the **New Library Item** ( ) button. Click **OK** to the style warning message. The **contest** style is in the shared style sheet, so we don't need to worry about that.

    NOTE: Sometimes the buttons in the **Assets** panel are grayed out when they shouldn't be. This buggy behavior can be worked around by going into the **Panel Menu** ( ) at the top right and choosing **New Library Item.**

20. The name **Untitled** appears in the bottom of the **Assets** panel. Change Untitled to **contest.** Now that we've set up the contest info as a Library item, it will be simple to add it to the rest of our pages.

21. In the **Assets** panel, click on the **contest** library item. The contest text will appear in the top half of the panel. Remember, don't worry that the preview does not reflect the styling.

22. Go to **File > Save All.**

23. Do a **File > Close All.**

24. In the **Files** panel, double-click **tips.html** to open it.

25. Place the cursor at the start of the heading **Tips for Summer.**

26. In the **Library** ( ) section of the **Assets** panel select **contest,** then click the **Insert** button at the bottom left of the panel.

CHANGING LIBRARY ITEMS

Oh no, this isn't the 19th anniversary, it's the 20th! We need to change it. Does that mean we have to go back and change every page with copyright text individually? Of course not—Dreamweaver's library function makes life easy.

1. In the **Library** ( ) section of the **Assets** panel, double-click on **contest** to open it. (Double-click the icon, instead of the name.)

2. The contest library item appears in a new window.

3. Change the year from 19 to **20.**

4. Go to **File > Save.** Dreamweaver kindly offers to update the library item wherever it appears on the site. Click **Update,** and now all of the pages with contest text will include the link!

5. **Close** the report that opens.

6. **Close** the **contest** library file so you are back in **tips.html** and can see the updated anniversary year. Nice!

7. Go to **File > Save All.**

8. Go to **File > Close All.**

Library Items 4D

        Single elements - use over & over again.

        Not good for rollovers (any script)

        when saving a Library Item -, only saving content not style

Key Command   - See all properties of an element

        Opt + Cmd + click

Box & Block

        Box - Padding   vs   Margin

              |

          Inside elements   Btwn elements

MORE CSS STYLING

Borders

Padding

Margin

ADDING FLASH TO A PAGE

Inserting Flash (.swf files)

Inserting Flash Video (.flv files)

MORE BEHAVIORS

Opening New Browser Windows

Setting the Position of a Pop-Up Window (Editing the JavaScript Code)

SPRY MENUS (DROP-DOWN MENUS)

Creating Spry Menus

Changing the Styling of Spry Menus

EXERCISE PREVIEW

> **Tips to Use All Year Long**
>
> • Keep your refrigerator and freezer full. That way they don't warm up as fast when you open the door and they have to work less. Just don't keep the door open too long when deciding what of all that food you want to eat.
> • Plant trees in the yard. They shade in the summer and break cold winds in the winter.
> • Clean the lint filter of your dryer after every load.
> • Close doors and heating/cooling vents in rooms that you aren't using.
> • Unless a recipe tells you otherwise, before putting hot food in the refrigerator, cool it to room temperature.
> • Defrost manual-defrost refrigerators and freezers when the frost is 1/4" thick.
> • Dry multiple loads of laundry immediately after one another. You'll use less energy because the dryer is already heated.
> • Dishwashers use less water than hand washing dishes. Let the dishes air dry to save even more.
> • If you're away from home for more than a few days, turn down the water heater.

EXERCISE OVERVIEW

CSS allows you to fine tune the elements of your layout. In this exercise we'll precisely edit our list elements — controlling the space between lines, adding a rule below the heading, and reducing the left indent of the bulleted list.

1. If you completed the previous exercises (4A–4D) you should have a Dreamweaver site defined for **NY Solar** so you can skip over the following sidebar. If you haven't finished the previous exercises, do the following sidebar.

> **IF YOU DID NOT DO THE PREVIOUS EXERCISES (4A–4D)**
>
> 1. In Dreamweaver, go to **Site > Manage Sites.**
> 2. If you see **yourname-NY Solar** select it and click **Remove.** (Click **Yes** to confirm.)
> 3. Click **Done** to close this dialog.
> 4. Go to **Site > New Site.**
> 5. A **Site Definition** dialog will open. Click the **Advanced** tab at the top.
> 6. For **Site name** enter **yourname-NY Solar.**
> 7. Next to **Local root folder**, click on the folder (📁) icon and navigate until you get to **Class Files.** Go into the **yourname-Dreamweaver Class** folder and
> 8. **(WINDOWS)**: Double-click on the subfolder **NY Solar Ready for More CSS.** Then click the **Select** button. Click **OK** to finish defining the site.
> 9. **(MAC)**: Select the **NY Solar Ready for More CSS** folder and click **Choose.** Click **OK** to finish defining the site.

2. In the **Files** panel double-click **tips.html.**

ZEROING OUT THE DEFAULTS

The site is looking pretty nice, but the spacing between the headings and lists needs some tweaking. To get a clear picture of how each element is affecting it, we're going to zero out the default padding and margins and go from there.

1. In the **CSS Styles** panel click **New CSS Rule** (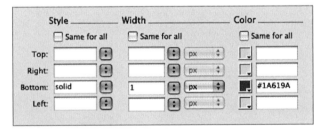) and specify the following:
   - Set the **Selector Type** to **Tag.**
   - In the middle next to **Selector Name** type **ul.**
   - Under **Rule Definition** make sure **styles-main.css** is chosen

   Click **OK.**

2. On the left side, select the **Box** section.

3. For BOTH **Padding** and **Margin, Same for all** should be checked. Make them **0.**
   NOTE: Padding and margins add space to objects in different places.
   When thinking of a box, **padding** is **inside** the box and **margin** is **outside** the box.

4. Click **OK.**

5. Look at the list. The bullets hang out too far to the left, but we'll fix that soon. Right now we are removing the default space, that way we can put back specifically how much we want in a moment.

6. In the **CSS Styles** panel, double-click the **h2** rule to edit it.

7. On the left, select the **Box** section.

8. Make sure **Same for all** is checked and enter **0** for **Padding** and **Margin,** then click **Apply** to preview the change. Do NOT click OK yet!

BORDER AND SPACING

Now that we have a fresh start, let's start building up the spacing.

1. If you closed the **h2** style, double-click it again in the **CSS Styles** panel.

2. On the left side, select the **Border** section and set the following:

	Style		Width			Color	
	☐ Same for all		☐ Same for all			☐ Same for all	
Top:		⬍		⬍	px ⬍	☐	
Right:		⬍		⬍	px ⬍	☐	
Bottom:	solid	⬍	1	⬍	px ⬍	■	#1A619A
Left:		⬍		⬍	px ⬍	☐	

3. Click the **Apply** button to see the border.

4. On the left side, select the **Box** section.

5. Under **Padding,** uncheck **Same for all** and for **Bottom,** enter **3.**

6. Click the **Apply** button and watch what happens. Bottom Padding adds space between the text and border. Think of the border as the edge of the "box" so padding is added **inside** of it.

7. Under **Margin,** uncheck **Same for all,** and for **Bottom,** enter **5.**

8. Click the **Apply** button and watch what happens. Bottom Margin adds space after the border. Since the border is the edge of the "box," margin spacing is **outside.**

9. Under **Margin,** for **Top** enter **25** and click **OK.**

10. In the **CSS Styles** panel, double-click the **li** rule to edit it.

11. On the left side, click on **Box.**

12. Under **Padding,** set **0** for all.

13. Under **Margin,** set **0** for all.

14. Then under **Margin,** uncheck **Same for all** and for **Left,** enter **17** and click **Apply.**

15. Under **Margin,** for **Bottom** enter **3** and click **Apply.**

16. Click **OK.**

17. **Preview** the page and enjoy the enhanced readability of the new spacing. So much better.

(**OPTIONAL BONUS, IF YOU HAVE EXTRA TIME**)

- Edit the **p** style (p stands for the paragraph tags).
- Give it **10px** of **Bottom Margin, 10px Top Margin,** and **0** Left and Right.
- You can see the effect on the two paragraphs of text at the bottom of the page.

Spry → Behavior using Ajax (instead of Javascript)

Flash

    Insert FLV   - Progressive Download...

    Attributes of new window when clicking on Flash video on page.

        Behaviors > Open Browser Window → Flash.html
                                         Set width + height.
                                         (Add 20 pix padding
                                          around original video)

              3rd party resource
JW Player - program for Flash - can resize window of video

YouTube → can copy + paste from YouTube. has an Embed script.
        select div go to code + paste script w/in div tags.

EXERCISE PREVIEW

EXERCISE OVERVIEW

These days, Flash video is the most popular video format on the web. YouTube uses it, so why not you? We'll show you how to properly add Flash video to your site.

PREVIEWING THE FINAL GOAL

1. To get an idea of the finished project, go to **File > Open.**

2. In the **yourname-Dreamweaver Class** folder, go into the **Woofing Cookies** folder and open **videos-finished.html.**

3. Hit **F12** (WINDOWS) or **Option–F12** (MAC) to preview in a browser.

4. Click on the Cookie Monster logo at the top left of the page. The eyes should animate and you should hear the cookie monster munching on a cookie.

5. Also click on any of the four thumbnail images to watch the videos.

6. When finished, close the browser.

7. Return to Dreamweaver and close the document.

DEFINING THE WOOFING COOKIES SITE

1. Go to **Site > New Site.**

2. If it's not already selected, click on the **Advanced** tab at the top.

3. For **Site name** enter **yourname woofing cookies.**

4. Next to **Local root folder** click the folder (🗀) icon and in the **yourname-Dreamweaver Class** folder:

   (WINDOWS): Double-click on the subfolder **Woofing Cookies.**
      Click the **Select** button.
      Click **OK** to finish defining the site.

   (MAC): Select the **Woofing Cookies** folder and click **Choose.**
      Click **OK** to finish defining the site.

5. In the **Files** panel, double-click **videos-start.html** to open it.

6. Do a **File > Save As** and name the file **videos.html**.

INSERT THE FLASH LOGO

1. At the top left of the page, place the cursor in the text **insert flash logo here.**

2. **Ctrl–A** (WINDOWS) or **Cmd–A** (MAC) to select all the text.

3. Delete the text.

4. Go to **Insert > Media > SWF**.

5. In the dialog that appears, click the **Site Root** button.

6. Go into the **flash** folder and double-click **woofing-cookies-logo.swf.**
   If an Object Tag Accessibility Attributes dialog opens, just click **OK**.

7. The Flash content will appear as a gray box with a Flash icon (⌁) in the center.

8. If using **Internet Explorer** on the PC, go to **Commands >
   Insert Mark of the Web.**

9. Hit **F12** (WINDOWS) or **Option–F12** (MAC) to preview in a browser.
   NOTE: You have to click on Cookie Monster to start the sound and animation.

10. **Save** the file.
    NOTE: When doing this on a new site you may be told that a
    Scripts/AC_RunActiveContent.js folder/file has been added to the site.
    Just click **OK**. The message is reminding you to upload that file to the webserver.

INSERTING FLASH VIDEO

1. Go to **File > New** and set the following:
   • On the far left, choose **Blank Page.**
   • Page Type: **HTML**
   • Layout: **None**

   Click **Create.**

2. **Save** the file as **city-video.html.**

3. At the top of the document window next to **Title:**
   type in **Music Video: In The City**

4. Open the **CSS Styles** panel **(Window > CSS Styles).**

5. Click the **Attach Style Sheet** (▦) button towards the bottom right.

6. Click the **Browse** button and in the **Woofing Cookies** folder
   choose **styles-video.css**.

7. Hit **Choose** and/or **OK** until you are out of all the dialog boxes.

8. The background color of the document should now be black.

9. We'd like to have our movie in the center of the page. In the **Properties** panel, press the **CSS** (⬛ css) button to make sure you are editing the CSS properties.

10. In the **Properties** panel **Targeted Rule** should be set to **Body.** This indicates that we are editing the Body style in our style sheet.

11. Click the center align button in the **Properties** panel (☰). Now all pages that use this style sheet will automatically be centered.

12. Go to **Insert > Media > FLV.**

13. In the dialog that appears:
    • Leave **Video type** set to **Progressive Download Video.**
    • Next to **URL**, click the **Browse** button.
      – In the dialog that appears click the **Site Root** button.
      – Go into the **videos** folder and double-click **in-the-city.flv** to select it.
    • Next to **Skin**, choose any of the three **Clear** or **Corona** skins that you like. These are your playback controls.
    • Next to **Width** and **Height**, make sure **Constrain** is **checked** and click the **Detect Size** button.
    • Check **Auto play.**

14. Click **OK.**

15. If using **Internet Explorer** on the PC, go to **Commands > Insert Mark of the Web.**

16. **Save** the file.

17. **Preview** in a browser. The video should start playing immediately, groovy!

(**OPEN VIDEO CLIPS IN A NEW BROWSER WINDOW**)

Now we can put this video page in a new browser window when the user clicks a thumbnail image.

1. Close the file with the Flash video, so you are back in **videos.html.**

2. Select the **top left** video thumbnail image above **MUSIC VIDEO: IN THE CITY.**

3. Go to **Window > Behaviors.** This opens the **Behaviors** section of the **Tag Inspector** panel.

4. Click the ⊞ and choose **Open Browser Window.**

5. In the dialog that appears, enter the following:
   – **URL to display**: Click **Browse** and choose **city-video.html** in the
   Woofing Cookies folder.
   – Window width: **370**
   – Window height: **253**
   – Attributes: check **Resize handles**
   – Leave **Window Name** blank.
   – Click **OK.**

6. **Save** the file, **Preview** in the web browser and click on the thumbnail image to see the movie open in a new window.

> **OPTIONAL: ADDING THE THREE REMAINING "POP-UP" VIDEOS**

There are three more video thumbnails on the page. If time permits and you'd like more practice, you can create three new pages for each of these videos. Then link each thumbnail image to the video page using the open browser window behavior.

1. Go to **File > New** and create a new, blank HTML document with no preset layout.

2. Save the file as **live-video.html**.

3. At the top of the page next to **Title**, type in **Music Video : Jet Plane (Live)**

4. Open the **CSS Styles** panel (**Window > CSS Styles**) and attach (🔗) **styles-video.css**.

   The background should be black and the cursor should be blinking in the center. Sweet!

5. Go to **Insert > Media > FLV.**

6. In the dialog:

   • Leave **Video Type** set to **Progressive Download Video**.
   • Next to **URL**, click the **Browse** button. In the **videos** subfolder select **jet-plane-on-scott-and-gary-1985.flv** and hit OK ⬭WINDOWS⬭ or Choose ⬭MAC⬭.
   • Next to **Skin**, choose the same type of skin you chose earlier.
   • Next to **Width** and **Height**, make sure **Constrain** is **checked** and click the **Detect Size** button.
   • Check **Auto play.**

7. Click **OK.**

8. If using **Internet Explorer** on the PC, go to **Commands > Insert Mark of the Web.**

9. **Save** the file.

10. Close the file so you are back in **videos.html**.

11. Select the **top right** thumbnail image above **LIVE PERFORMANCE: JET PLANE.**

12. Go to **Window > Behaviors.**

13. Click the ⊞ and choose **Open Browser Window.**

14. In the dialog that appears, enter the following:
    – **URL to display:** Click **Browse** and choose **live-video.html** in the
      Woofing Cookies folder.
    – Window Width: **370**
    – Window Height: **253**
    – Attributes: check **Resize handles**
    – Leave **Window name** blank.
    – Click **OK.**

15. **Save** the file and **Preview** in the web browser.

(**OPTIONAL BONUS, IF YOU HAVE EXTRA TIME**)

To finish the final two videos, try your hand at going through the process on
your own. Here's a review of the steps:

• **Create** a blank, **new HTML** document and **save** it into the
  Woofing Cookies folder.
• **Attach** the **styles-video.css** stylesheet.
• Center the cursor and **Insert > Media > FLV.**
• Browse for the appropriate video from the **videos** folder.
• Choose a **Skin** and click **Detect Size** before hitting OK.
• If using **Internet Explorer** on the PC, go to
  Commands > Insert Mark of the Web.
• **Save** the new file.
• Return to **videos.html**.
• Select the thumbnail image and add the **Open Browser Window** Behavior.
• Browse to select the video page, then set: Window Width and Height and
  check **Resize handles**.
• Save **videos.html** and **Preview** your work!

AJAX - JavaScript +XML   Spry is
    Can load data more seamlessly.

EXERCISE PREVIEW

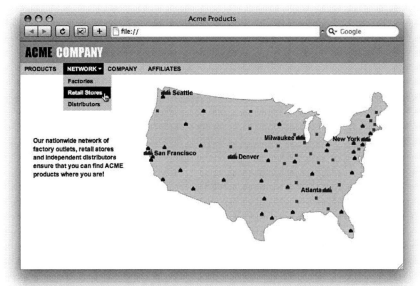

EXERCISE OVERVIEW

Dreamweaver includes tools for easily making interactive menus. The technology behind it is called Spry, which is fast to load and can be customized to fit the look of your site. We'll walk you through creating a simple menu that links to other pages in the site.

PREVIEWING THE FINISHED PRODUCT

1. Let's take a look at what we want to accomplish. Go to **File > Open** and from the **Acme Finished** folder open the file called **index.html.**

2. **Preview** the page.

3. The menu on the page was created using one of Dreamweaver's Spry Widgets. The Spry framework uses JavaScript and CSS to drive interactive functions. Mouse over the **Network** button near the top of the page to launch a drop-down menu. Try out the links if you like.

   PC Internet Explorer users: A yellow alert bar appears at the top of the page. You must click the yellow bar and choose **Allow Blocked Content** to get the menu to function properly. (This only happens when previewing the file locally.)

4. Back in Dreamweaver, close all the open files by going to **File > Close All.**

DEFINING THE ACME SITE

Spry menus require JavaScript and CSS files that Dreamweaver will add into your site. So that Dreamweaver knows where to add them, let's define a site.

1. In Dreamweaver, choose **Site > New Site.**

2. Click the **Advanced** tab at the top.

3. Under **Site Name** enter **yourname-Acme.**

4. Under **Local Root Folder,** click on the folder (📁) icon.

5. In the **Class Files** folder, go into **yourname-Dreamweaver Class** and select **Acme Started.**

   (WINDOWS): You'll have to open the folder so it says Select: **Acme** at the bottom of the window. Hit the **Select** button. Then hit **OK.**

   (MAC): Hit **Choose.** Then hit **OK.**

6. Go to the **Files** panel and double-click **index.html** to open it. This file doesn't yet have the menu but you'll create it momentarily!

ADDING THE SPRY WIDGET AND EDITING THE MAIN MENU ITEM TEXT

1. In the gray row just beneath the ACME COMPANY logo, place the cursor in the text **Menu Goes Here.**

2. To select all the text press **Ctrl–A** (WINDOWS) or **Cmd–A** (MAC).

3. Press **Delete.** (Be careful NOT to click anywhere! Until you insert the menu, clicking back into this layer will be almost impossible. The layer's **auto** height will shrink up to nothing since there is no content currently in the layer.)

4. In the **Insert** panel choose the **Spry** tab.

5. Click the **Spry Menu Bar** (🖼) button (5th from the right).

6. A **Spry Menu Bar** dialog will open. Select the **Horizontal** layout and hit **OK.**

7. A menu named **MenuBar1** will appear. We'll use the **Properties** panel to update it.

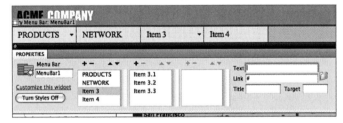

NOTE: As in the example above, you're going to highlight each of the Items in the first column, then update the **Text** field on the far right of the **Properties** panel.

8. With **Item 1** selected in the first column of the **Properties** panel, find the area on the right side that says **Text** and change Item 1 to **PRODUCTS.**

9. Select **Item 2** in the first column, on the right change **Text** to **NETWORK.**

10. Select **Item 3,** and change **Text** to **COMPANY.**

11. Select **Item 4**, and change **Text** to **AFFILIATES**.

    NOTE: **Text** is what the user sees in the menu, and **Link** is the URL where they will be taken. We'll add the Links later on.

12. Save what you have so far **(File > Save).**

    NOTE: A **Copy Dependent Files** dialog should pop up to alert you to the JavaScript, CSS and image files that Dreamweaver needs to link to the page in order for this menu to work properly. Click **OK**.

13. Dreamweaver has copied the required files into the site folder. Take a look in the **Files** panel. You should see a new **SpryAssets** folder. If it didn't appear, click the **Refresh** ($\boxed{C}$) button at the top of the **Files** panel. Now we're ready to proceed.

EDITING THE SUBMENU ITEMS

1. To edit the menu we must first select it. Click anywhere in the menu text.

2. In the Quick Tag Selector at the bottom of the document window click on **<ul.MenubarHorizontal#MenuBar1>.**

3. In the **Properties** panel select **PRODUCTS** in the first column.

4. In the column directly to the right, you'll see three submenu items. Let's delete them. Select **Item 1.1** and click the **Remove** ($\boxed{-}$) button **3** times to delete all 3 items:

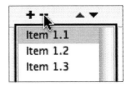

5. Select **COMPANY** in the first column of the **Properties** panel.

6. In the column to the right, select **Item 3.1** and click the **Remove** ($\boxed{-}$) button. You'll get a warning message to let you know that the menu has "children," or more submenu items. Go ahead and click **OK** to delete everything.

7. Highlight **Item 3.2** and click the **Remove** ($\boxed{-}$) button twice to delete the rest of these submenu items.

8. Let's add submenu items to NETWORK. In the first column select **NETWORK**.

9. In the column to the right, click the **Add** ($\boxed{+}$) button three times to add three new **Untitled Items.**

10. Select the first **Untitled Item.**

11. At the right of the **Properties** panel set the following:
    Text: **Factories**
    Link: **factories.html**

12. For the remaining two **Untitled Item**s, change **Text** and **Link** to the following:

Text:	Link:
Retail Stores	**stores.html**
Distributors	**distributors.html**

13. Do a **File > Save.**

14. Hit **F12** ⟨WINDOWS⟩ or **Option–F12** ⟨MAC⟩ to preview it in a browser.
    (PC users may want to use Firefox to avoid the IE yellow bar security hassles.)
    Try out the menu. Once you click on the links, you'll have to use the browser's
    Back button to return to the first page because we haven't added the menu to
    the other pages yet. But so far, so good!

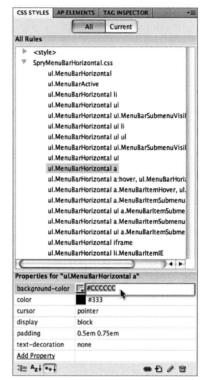

(**MAKING STYLE CHANGES TO THE MENU**)

The menu is operational but doesn't suit our design as well as it
could. We can update the style of text and the color of the menu and
rollovers by updating the CSS that Dreamweaver created for us when
we inserted the Spry Menu.

1. Go back to Dreamweaver and open the **CSS Styles** panel
   (Window > CSS Styles).

2. You will see the **SpryMenuBarHorizontal.css** style sheet that is
   attached to the document. Expand it to see the long list of styles that
   control the look of the menu.

3. As shown to the right, find the style called **ul.MenuBarHorizontal a**
   and select it.

4. With the **ul.MenuBarHorizontal a** style selected, at the bottom of the
   panel change the **background-color** to **#CCCCCC.**

5. Let's change the font and a few other settings. To get to the
   settings, at the top of the **CSS Styles** panel double-click the style
   ul.MenuBarHorizontal a.

6. In the dialog that opens make the following changes:

   Font-family: **Arial, Helvetica, sans-serif**
   Font-size: **11 (px)**
   Font-weight: **bold**
   Color: **#000000** (black)

   Click **OK.**

7. Now let's change the background color of the menu when the mouse rolls over
   the item. To do this we must make the change to two styles. First, in the **CSS
   Styles** panel, select the style just **below ul.MenuBarHorizontal a.**

8. At the bottom of the panel change the **background-color** from **#33C** to **#274463.**

9. Select the next style down in the list (the 2nd style below **ul.MenuBarHorizontal a**).

10. In the bottom of the panel, again change **background-color** from **#33C** to **#274463.**

11. Whew. Do a **File > Save All.** (This saves the webpage to which you added the menu as well as the CSS file that was opened when you started editing it.)

12. Hit **F12** (**WINDOWS**) or **Option–F12** (**MAC**) to preview it in a browser and try out the new, stylized menu! If the color hasn't updated you may need to click the browser's **Refresh** button.

CHANGING THE WIDTH OF THE MAIN MENU ITEMS

When doing the following sections read the style names carefully so you edit the correct styles.

1. The menus are a bit wide aren't they? We can fix that. In the **CSS Styles** panel select the **3rd** style from the top (named **ul.MenuBarHorizontal li**).

2. At the bottom of the panel change the width to **auto.**

3. The arrow is now too close to the text. To fix that **double-click** the style named **ul.MenuBarHorizontal a** ← Be careful to get the right style name!

4. In the dialog that opens, on the left click on **Box.**

5. Increase the **Padding, Right** to **1.3** (ems). Click **OK.**

6. Do a **File > Save All.**

7. Hit **F12** (**WINDOWS**) or **Option–F12** (**MAC**) to preview it in a browser. You may have to click the browser's **Refresh** button to make sure you see the change.

CHANGING THE WIDTH OF THE SUBMENU ITEMS

1. The submenus are still too wide. To fix that we'll need to edit two styles. First, in the **CSS Styles** panel select the **4th** style from the **top** (named **ul.MenuBarHorizontal ul**).

2. At the bottom of the panel, next to **width** change 8.2 (ems) to **5.8** (ems).

3. Now select the style named **ul.MenuBarHorizontal ul li.**

4. At the bottom of the panel, next to **width** change 8.2 (ems) to **5.8** (ems).

5. Do a **File > Save All.**

6. Hit **F12** (WINDOWS) or **Option–F12** (MAC) to preview it in a browser. You may have to click the browser's **Refresh** button to make sure you see the change.

(**OPTIONAL BONUS, IF YOU HAVE EXTRA TIME**)

If you finish early, try your hand at copying the menu into the other three pages: **factories.html, stores.html** and **distributors.html.**

To put the menu you just created onto other pages:

• Select the menu by clicking once on the blue tab that says
  Spry Menu Bar: MenuBar1 (Don't see the blue tab? Click inside the menu text.
  Then click **<ul.MenubarHorizontal#MenuBar1>** in the Quick Tag Selector.)

• Copy it **(Ctrl–C** (WINDOWS) or **Cmd–C** (MAC)**).**

• Go to another page and click into the gray row with the text
  Menu Goes Here.

• Select All **(Ctrl–A** (WINDOWS) or **Cmd–A** (MAC)**).**

• Delete the text.

• **Paste** in the menu **(Ctrl–V** (WINDOWS) or **Cmd–V** (MAC)**).**

GOING LIVE WITH YOUR WEBSITE

What is a Webhost and how does it work?

Entering the Remote Site information for your site

Uploading your files to a webserver via FTP in Dreamweaver

CREATING FORMS

Text Fields

Radio Buttons

Checkboxes

Menus

Hidden Fields

Linking to Server Side Scripts to Process Form Data

Submitting & Testing Forms

SITE MANAGEMENT (CHECKING & MAINTAINING FILES/LINKS)

Creating Folders

Renaming Files

Moving Files

Checking Links

Locating Orphan Files

JUMP MENUS

Creating a long list of links in a small space

Copying and pasting code for quick edits

Opening jump menu links in a new window

1. Domain Name
2. Host - Host   → Go Daddy
         Directory   Dream Host
         Login
           Pswd

EXERCISE PREVIEW

EXERCISE OVERVIEW

In this exercise you'll upload a website to a remote server so you can see how to take the work you've done in Dreamweaver and actually put it live on the web. If you're taking a Noble Desktop instructor-led class, you will be supplied with the connection information, otherwise you can sign up for a free account with Tripod on your own. If you create your own account, it's free and yours to keep, so it can be your first website if you don't already have one.

thejivefactory.com

IF YOU'RE IN A NOBLE DESKTOP INSTRUCTOR-LED CLASS

1. The instructor will supply you with a user name and password.
   So you don't forget them, write them down (you'll need them later):

   Username: *nobledesktop01*   *tripod*

   Password: *student*

2. Skip the section below and continue with the section titled **Defining the Site**.

IF YOU'RE WORKING FROM THE BOOK AT YOUR OFFICE OR HOME

1. Open a web browser and go to **http://www.tripod.com**. *←use for practice at home*

2. In the center of the page, if you see a green **Start Now!** button, click it and move on to the next step.
   If you don't see it, someone has already signed up on this computer, so:
   • Look for the **Hello, username!** message at the top left of the page.
   • Click the **Logout** link to the right of the user name.
   • The homepage will refresh automatically; click the green **Start Now!** button.

3. Look for the plan that says **Tripod Free.**
   Click the green **Sign Up** button under that.

4. Now a new page with an orange **Sign Up** button will load. Click the button!

5. Read the following before filling out the form:
   • Choose your user name carefully as it will be part of your website address
     which will be **http://username.tripod.com**
   • So you don't forget them, write them down (you'll need them later):

   Username: _____

   Password: _____

6. Complete the rest of the form and click **I Agree** at the bottom. You will be sent to
   a page asking if you are ready to get started. Ignore it and go to the next step.

7. Let's see what your website looks like right now.
   Go to **http://username.tripod.com**

8. This is just the default index page. Now switch back to Dreamweaver.

(DEFINING THE SITE)

1. Before you can upload the files to your webserver we need to define a site.
   In Dreamweaver, go to **Site > New Site.**

2. If it's not already selected, click on the **Advanced** tab at the top.
   (Don't click OK until we say so!)

3. For **Site name** enter **yourname-Public Handicapper.**

4. Next to **Local Root Folder** click the folder (📁) icon and
   in the **yourname-Dreamweaver Class** folder:

   (WINDOWS): Double-click on the subfolder **Public Handicapper.**
           Click the **Select** button.

   (MAC): Select the **Public Handicapper** folder and click **Choose.**

5. Under HTTP Address:
   – In Class: enter **http://www.thejivefactory.com/username**
   – Home/Office: enter **http://username.tripod.com**

6. On the left of the window, click **Remote Info.**

7. From the **Access** menu choose **FTP** and enter the following:

   FTP Host:
   – In Class: **ftp.thejivefactory.com**
   – Home/Office: **ftp.tripod.com** (we found this information in Tripod's help
     system)

   Host directory: Leave blank

Login:
– In Class: **username@thejivefactory.com**
– Home/Office: enter the **Username** you selected earlier

Password: enter the **Password** you selected or were given earlier

8. Click the **Test** button.

9. If Dreamweaver announces it has successfully connected, click **OK**.

   If Dreamweaver cannot make a connection:
   • Double-check your user name.
   • Double-check your password.
   • Make sure there are no extra spaces.

   If all else fails:
   • Select **Use passive FTP**

10. When done click **OK**.

11. The **Files** panel (shown below) should appear.

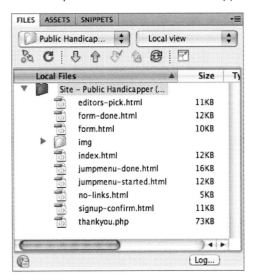

(GETTING FAMILIAR WITH THE WEBSITE & CUSTOMIZING CONTENT)

Let's see what you're about to upload and take a moment to edit one of the pages in the site to make it your own.

1. In the **Files** panel double-click **index.html** to open it.

2. Hit **F12** (WINDOWS) or **Option–F12** (MAC) to preview the page in a browser.

3. Not all the navbar buttons are linked yet, but the **Editors' Picks** is. Go ahead and click on it to test it out.

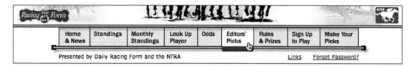

4. Let's customize this Editors' Picks page. Return to Dreamweaver and in the **Files** panel double-click **editors-pick.html** to open it.

5. In the middle of the page, next to **Editor:** replace **PutYourNameHere** with **your own name**.

6. Just below, you should see some text that says **My Pick is.** Pick a horse by deleting the names you don't want!

7. **Save** the file.

GOING LIVE

1. Let's expand the **Files** panel to show more information. Near the top right of the panel click the **Expand/Collapse** (⊡) button to expand it to the full **Files** window (it will fill up the whole screen on the PC).

2. Click the **Connect** (🔌) button towards the top left of the **Files** window.

3. On the left is the LIVE site and on the right is your local computer.
   – Home/Office (Tripod site): If you have an **index.htm** page on the left, that is Tripod's default home page. Click on it and hit **Delete**. If Dreamweaver asks to confirm the deletion, just agree.

4. Click on **index.html** in the right side of the window.

5. Hold **Control** (WINDOWS) or **Command** (MAC) and click on **editors-pick.html** to also select it.

6. You should now have **index.html** and **editors-pick.html** selected on the right side.

7. At the top of the **Files** window click the **Put Files** (⬆) button.

8. When you get a message asking if you want to include dependent files click **Yes.** If you get a message about Synchronization info just click **Yes to All.**

9. The Background File Activity window will automatically close to indicate that the file transfer is complete. That's it, you have a live site! To see the remote files on the web, switch to a browser and go to:

   – In Class: **http://www.thejivefactory.com/username**
   – Home/Office: **http://yourusername.tripod.com**

10. Click the **Editors' Picks** button in the navbar to see your pick, wooohooo!

IF YOUR IMAGES DID NOT GET UPLOADED

If your images and other dependent files did not get uploaded you'll need to set a preference to make sure that they do.

1. Go into **Edit > Preferences** (WINDOWS) or **Dreamweaver > Preferences** (MAC).

2. On the left click on the **Site** category.

3. Next to **Dependent Files**, check both boxes.

4. Click **OK.**

5. Make sure **index.html** and **editors-pick.html** are both selected.

6. At the top of the **Files** window click the **Put Files** (⬆) button.

7. When you get a message asking if you want to include dependent files click **Yes.**

8. The images should get automatically uploaded.

9. Go back to the live site and check it out.

MAKING CHANGES

To make changes later, you change the local files on your computer. Then:

• **Connect** (🔌) to the remote site (through the **Files** panel as you just did above).

• Select the updated files in the **Local Files** list (the right side of the window).

• Click the **Put** (⬆) button.

The new files will replace the older files. Just remember, whatever you do to the live remote site happens instantly and CANNOT be undone, so upload carefully!

Forms.

CGI - Common Gateway Interface   (PERL, C++)

host sends to: cgi-bin/   ] given to us from host

Tell form what to do w/ info.
        select form - Properties - Action:

Different for {   /scripts/form-handler.php →Jivef
each host.   {   /bin/script_library/form_handler_mail →tripod

Edgeweb → for e-commerce hosting
        hosting.net

EXERCISE PREVIEW

EXERCISE OVERVIEW

You'll find a form on almost every website. In this exercise we'll show you how to create all the typical form elements like checkboxes, text fields and menus. We'll also show you how to submit the form to a script on the webserver that will process the form information and send you an email, put it into a database, etc.

You'll continue working with the **Public Handicapper** site you defined in the previous exercise. If you don't have that site defined, refer to the previous exercise for the site definition info.

1. We're going to make a form for new users to sign up. To see what the finished form should look like, go to the **Files** panel and double-click **form-done.html** to open it.

2. Hit **F12** (WINDOWS) or **Option–F12** (MAC) to preview the page in a browser.

3. Close the browser and return to Dreamweaver.

FORM PREFERENCES

1. Go into **Edit > Preferences** (WINDOWS) or **Dreamweaver > Preferences** (MAC).

2. On the left click on the **Accessibility** category.

3. Under **Show attributes when inserting**, deselect (uncheck) all boxes.

4. Click **OK**.

SETTING UP THE FORM

1. In the **Files** panel, double-click **form.html** to open it.

2. To make sure the form is visible when you insert it, go into **View > Visual Aids** and make sure **Invisible Elements** is checked.

3. The top and bottom parts of the page are already created; you'll insert a form between them. Click into the empty area in the middle of the page below **Presented by Daily Racing Form and the NTRA** and above the bottom navigation table.

4. Because you're creating a form, you'll need the forms objects to be displayed. In the **Insert** panel, at the top, click on the **Forms** tab.

5. Click the **Form** (▫) button (the first button).
   You'll see a red bounding box appear. For the form to be processed correctly, you must make sure to place all content inside the form field.

6. The cursor should already be in the red form box, so go into **Insert > Table**.

7. Give the table these specs:

Rows: **10**	Columns: **2**
Table width: **580 (pixels)**	
Border thickness: **0**	
Cell padding: **3**	
Cell spacing: **0**	
Header: **None**	

   Don't do anything with the Accessibility options.
   Click **OK**.

8. With the table still selected, in the **Properties** panel set **Align** to **Center**.

9. Go to **View > Visual Aids** and make sure **Table Widths** is checked.

10. To set the column widths properly, select the divider between the two columns of the table and drag to the left until the number above the **left** column of the Table Width preview reads **200** (the right will read 368).

ADDING CONTENT TO THE TABLE AND STYLING THE TEXT

1. In the top, left column type: **Sign Up To Play!**

2. Directly below this cell, type: **Contact Info**

3. Select the **top row** by clicking and dragging across both columns from left to right.

4. Merge them by clicking the **Merge Cells** () button in the bottom left corner of the **Properties** panel.

5. Do the same for the second row.

6. The top two rows of the table should look as shown below.

580 ▾		
200 ▾	368 ▾	
Sign Up To Play!		
Contact Info		

7. Open the **CSS Styles** panel **(Window > CSS Styles).**

8. You'll see some internal styles already defined for the document. We need to create some new custom styles for the form. Click **New CSS Rule** ( ) at the bottom of the **CSS Styles** panel and set the following.

   • set the **Selector Type** to **Class**
   • in the middle under **Selector Name**, type **form-head**
   • under **Rule Definition** make sure **This document only** is selected.

   Click **OK.**

9. In the **CSS Rule Definition** dialog that appears set the following:

   Font-size: **20 (px)**
   Font-weight: **bold**
   Color: **#E61000**

   Click **OK.**

10. To apply this style, click in the top cell (where you typed "Sign Up To Play!") and in the Quick Tag Selector at the bottom of the window click the `<td>` tag.

11. In the **Properties** panel press the HTML (`<> HTML`) button, then from the **Class** menu choose **form-head.**

12. Let's create a style for the section headings. Click **New CSS Rule** ( ) at the bottom of the **CSS Styles** panel.
    • set the **Selector Type** to **Class**
    • in the middle under **Selector Name**, type **form-sectionhead**
    • under **Rule Definition** make sure **This document only** is selected.

    Click **OK.**

13. Don't click OK until we say! In the **CSS Rule Definition** dialog set the following:

    Font-size: **12 (px)**
    Font-weight: **bold**

14. On the left, click on **Box**.

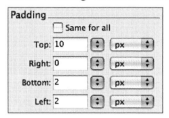

15. Under **Padding, uncheck Same for All** and enter the settings shown below.

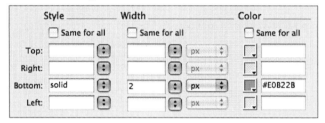

16. Finally, let's add a rule beneath the text. On the left click on **Border.**

17. Enter the settings shown below.

18. Click **OK**.

19. To apply the style, click in the second row where you typed **Contact Info.**

20. In the Quick Tag Selector at the bottom of the window click the `<td>` tag.

21. In the **Properties** panel from the **Class** menu choose **form-sectionhead.**

22. Go to **File > Save.**

(ADDING TEXT FIELDS TO THE FORM)

1. In the two left-hand cells directly **below** the **Contact Info** row, add the following text:
   Name:
   Email:

2. To select those two cells, click in the **Name** cell and drag down to the **Email** cell.

3. Using the **Properties** panel, set **Horz** to **Right.** (As shown below.)

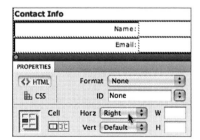

4. Click in the cell in the right column next to **Name.**

5. Go to the **Insert** panel and click the **Text Field** ([I☐]) button (second button).

6. In the **Properties** panel make the **Char width 40.**

7. Select the text field in the cell and **Copy** and **Paste** it into the cell underneath.

8. We need to name each text field so when we receive the data we'll know what the info is. Click on the **top text field.**

9. At the left of the **Properties** panel see where it says **textfield** in a white box? As shown on the right, change this to **name** and hit **Enter** (WINDOWS) or **Return** (MAC).

10. Click on the text field next to **Email** (textfield2). Name this one **email.**

11. After all this work, press **Ctrl–S** (WINDOWS) or **Cmd–S** (MAC) to save this file.

12. Let's organize the table a bit by adding a new section heading and styling it the same as the first. Select the entire row just below Email.

13. Merge the two columns by clicking the **Merge Cells** (🔲) button in the bottom left of the **Properties** panel.

14. Click inside the newly created cell and type **Your Interests.**

15. In the Quick Tag Selector at the bottom of the window click the **<td>** tag to select the "Your Interests" cell.

16. In the **Properties** panel from the **Class** menu choose **form-sectionhead.**

17. Below "Your Interests," in the next empty left-hand cell, type this text:
    Experience Level:

18. In the succeeding left-hand cells, add the following text.
    What do you read?
    You go to the track:
    Tell us about yourself!

19. **Right** align all the text in these cells.

20. The table should now look as shown to the right:

21. **Save** what you've done so far.

*radio button name
if all same name, can only
select one. If diff. names,
use checkbox.*

Sign Up to Play!	
Contact Info	
Name:	
Email:	
Your Interests	
Experience Level:	
What do you read?	
You go to the track:	
Tell us about yourself!	

(ADDING RADIO BUTTONS)

1. Click in the cell to the right of **Experience Level.**

2. In the **Insert** panel, click on the **Radio** (⦿) button.

3. On the left of the **Properties** panel, under **Radio Button**, name it **level.**
    (You'll change the **Checked Value** later.)

4. Click to the **right** of the radio button and type **Expert.**

5. After **Expert**, type **two Ctrl–Shift–Spaces** (WINDOWS) or **two Option–Spaces** (MAC). These are special characters called non-breaking spaces, the only way to get text to move more than one space.

— only allowed 1 regular spad max.

6. **Copy** and **Paste** the first radio button over to the right of **Expert** and the spaces.

7. Type **Decent** next to the second radio button and then add **two Ctrl–Shift–Spaces** (WINDOWS) or two **Option–Spaces** (MAC).

8. **Ctrl–Drag** (WINDOWS) or **Option–Drag** (MAC) another copy of the first radio button over the right of **Decent** and the spaces.

9. Type **Complete Loser** next to this last radio button.

10. Because you copied these radio buttons, they have the same name and are therefore grouped. That means web surfers can only select one in that group. However, they need to have different values so you'll know which one they checked. Select the **Expert** radio button and in the **Properties** panel, next to **Checked value**, enter **expert**

11. Select the **Decent** radio button and enter **decent** next to **Checked value**.

12. Lastly, select the **Complete Loser** button and enter **loser** next to **Checked value**.

13. Let's select one of them by default. To make it **Decent**, select that button, and in the **Properties** panel, under **Initial State**, click on **Checked**. Now you're all set.

   ○ Expert ● Decent ○ Complete Loser

14. **Save** the file.

15. **Preview** in a browser, then switch back to Dreamweaver.

(ADDING CHECKBOXES)

1. Click into the cell next to **What do you read?**

2. In the **Insert** panel hit the **Checkbox** (☑) button.

3. Next to the checkbox type **Daily Racing Form** followed by **two Ctrl–Shift–Spaces** (WINDOWS) or **Option–Spaces** (MAC).

4. Select the checkbox.

5. In **Properties**, name it **publications** with a checked value of **Daily Racing Form**.

6. **Copy** and **Paste** the checkbox to the right.

7. After the new checkbox, type **Elle**. It should look like this:
   ☐ **Daily Racing Form**   ☐ **Elle**

8. Select the **Elle** checkbox.

9. Change its checked value to **Elle.**

10. The name has been renamed **publications2**. The name may be too long to see the 2, but it's there if you scroll/arrow through the name.

11. Delete the 2 at the end so it's just named **publications.**

12. **Save** and **Preview** the page in a web browser to make sure everything is cool. Then switch back to Dreamweaver.

ADDING MENUS & MULTI-LINE TEXT FIELDS

1. Click in the cell next to **You go to the track:**

2. In the **Insert** panel click the **List/Menu** ( ) button.

3. On the page, you'll see a menu appear in the cell. In the **Properties** panel click the **List Values** button.

4. In the dialog that appears, **Item Label** indicates what the viewer will actually see and select. **Value** is what the form returns to the webmaster when it's submitted. To switch fields and add new ones, just hit the **Tab** key. Type in the following:

Item Label:	Value:
Every Day it's Open	daily
Once a Year	yearly
Whenever I Feel Masochistic	masochistic

Can sort lists!

5. Click **OK**.

6. On the left of the **Properties** panel name the menu **howoftentrack**

7. Click in the cell to the right of **Tell us about yourself!**

8. In the **Insert** panel click the **Textarea** ( ) button.

9. In the **Properties** panel:
   • Name it **comments**
   • Make **Char width**: **38**
   • Make **Num Lines**: **5**

10. Click in the **Tell us about yourself!** cell.

11. In the **Properties** panel set **Vert** (Vertical align) to the **Top**.

12. **Save** and **Preview**. Then go back to Dreamweaver.

ADDING A SUBMIT BUTTON AND HIDDEN FIELDS

1. Click in the empty cell in last row, right column.

2. In the **Insert** panel click the **Button** ( ) icon.

3. The button will automatically come up as a **Submit** button. In the **Properties** panel, next to **Value**, type **Sign Me Up!** and hit **Enter** (WINDOWS) or **Return** (MAC) to kick it in.

4. In the Quick Tag Selector, click on the **<form>** tag.

5. In the **Properties** panel, under **Form ID** type **signup**.

CUSTOMIZING THE FORM FOR YOUR WEBHOST

1. The next steps depend on your webhost, either Tripod or the Noble provided host. Choose the column that is appropriate for you.

IF YOU'RE IN A NOBLE DESKTOP CLASS

1. In the field next to **Action** type **/scripts/form-handler.php**

2. Click in the empty cell to the left of the **Sign Me Up** button.

3. In the **Insert** panel click the **Hidden Field** ( ) button.

4. In the **Properties** panel name it **end_display.**

5. Next to **Value** type: **/username/thankyou.php**

6. Select the checkbox next to **Daily Racing Form.**

7. In the **Properties** panel, add square brackets after its name. It should read **publications[].**

8. Do the same to the checkbox next to Elle. Its name should also be **publications[].** Our script requires brackets at the end of the name of checkboxes. Every script is different, consult with your webhost.

IF YOU'RE WORKING AT HOME/OFFICE

1. In the field next to **Action** type: **/bin/script_library/form_handler_mail.**

2. Click in the empty cell to the left of the **Sign Me Up** button.

3. In the **Insert** panel click the **Hidden Field** ( ) button.

4. In the **Properties** panel name it **end_display.**

5. Next to **Value** type: **/signup-confirm.html**

6. Click to the right of the hidden field you just made, so the cursor is blinking there.

7. In the **Insert** panel click the **Hidden Field** ( ) button.

8. In the **Properties** panel name it **email_to.**

9. Next to **Value** type in your email address. This specifies the email address to which the form's contents will be sent. This field is hidden to the user but not to the script!

NOTES: The form gets submitted to a server-side script. Tripod provides this script. If you are using another webhost, you will need to check to see if they have provided a script, the file path to access it, and how exactly to use it. Since such a script resides on the server, you won't be able to test the form until you upload it to the web server. In our case, the hidden field **end_display** indicates the page you want to display as a "thank you" page once the form is submitted. You will "end" on that page.

2. **Save** the file.

UPLOAD AND TEST THE FORM

1. Open the **Files** panel **(Window > Files).**

2. If you do not see the **Remote** and **Local** file lists in the **Files** panel, near the top right of the panel click the **Expand/Collapse** ( ) button to expand it.

3. Click the **Connect** ( ) button at the top of the **Files** window.

4. Remember: on the left is the **LIVE** site and on the right are the local files. You are about to upload several files: the index page, the form and the confirmation page. Click once on **index.html** to select it.

5. Hold down **Ctrl** (WINDOWS) or **Cmd** (MAC) and, in the right (local) section of the panel, click on **form.html, signup-confirm.html,** and **thankyou.php** to select all the files at once.

6. At the top of the **Files** window click the **Put Files** (⬆) button.
   If you get a message asking if you want to include dependent files, click **No** (we already uploaded all the images needed in the past exercise).
   If you get a message about Synchronization info click **Yes to All.**

7. When the file transfer is complete, switch to a browser and go to:
   – In Class: **http://www.thejivefactory.com/username**
   – Home/Office: **http://yourusername.tripod.com**

8. Click the **Sign Up to Play** button in the navbar.

9. Fill out the form and hit **Sign Me Up**!

10. When the confirmation page loads:
    – **In Class:** The form info has been processed and passed to the thank you page. Normally that info would go into a database or get sent in an email, but in this case we've just passed it into a table so you can see that the form really did work.
    – **Home/Office:** You're ready to **check your email** for the form info. Look for a message in your Inbox from Tripod Form Mailer with the subject line **Results From Your Form.** Please note, that there seems to a bug in the free Tripod CGI script that causes only one of two possible checkbox values to be forwarded along with the form results. The script you acquire from your own host should have no problem correctly passing all your checkbox values.

11. If you're missing any of the fields of information, open up **form.html** and check the names to make sure you haven't made any mistakes. Refer to **form-done.html** if needed. Fix the names, re-upload **form.html**, then reload the webpage and try out the form again.

12. Success!

Site Management

Local Folder -

May want to have >1 folder

index   index

Index w/in each folder for a
subsection of that site.

Dragging files into new sub folders in DW will update links.

If you type url → folder name it will automatically
bring you to the index file

Always back up your files. Hackers can hack website.
Good idea to put on external hard-drive

When testing your sites - No homepage - (empty Page) - Faster to cut & paste urls

EXERCISE PREVIEW

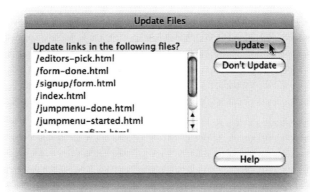

EXERCISE OVERVIEW

This exercise will introduce you to standard file maintenance such as renaming and moving files, checking for broken links, identifying and deleting unused files and compiling a list of external links.

1. Dreamweaver's site management features require a site to be defined. If you completed the previous exercises (6A & 6B) you should have a site defined for **Public Handicapper** so you can skip over the following sidebar. If you haven't finished the previous exercises (and therefore do not have a **Public Handicapper** site) do the following sidebar.

> ## IF YOU DID NOT DO THE PREVIOUS EXERCISES (6A & 6B)
>
> 1. In Dreamweaver, go to **Site > New Site.**
> 2. A **Site Definition** dialog will open. Click the **Advanced** tab at the top.
> 3. For **Site name** enter **yourname-Public Handicapper.**
> 4. Next to **Local root folder**, click on the folder (📁) icon and navigate until you get to **Class Files.** Go into the **yourname-Dreamweaver Class** folder and
>
>   (WINDOWS): Double-click on the subfolder **Public Handicapper.**
>   Then click the **Select** button. Click **OK** to finish defining the site.
>
>   (MAC): Select the **Public Handicapper** folder and click **Choose.**
>   Click **OK** to finish defining the site.

(CREATE A NEW FOLDER AND MOVE A FILE)

1. If it's not already open, go to the **Files** panel **(Window > Files).**

2. Select the local root **Site** folder (the green folder at the top of the list of files).

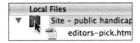

3. At the top right of the **Files** panel, go into the **Options menu** (▾≣) and choose **File > New Folder.** On the PC, if the **File** panel is full screen, you must first click the **Expand/Collapse** (⬚) button to turn it back into a panel.

4. A new, **untitled** folder will be put into the site. Name the folder **signup**.

5. Drag **form.html** into the new **signup** folder.

6. A dialog will appear to ask you if you want to update some links. Click the **Update** button. Dreamweaver has now fixed your links, awesome!

(RENAME A FILE)

Let's make **form.html** the "home page" of the **signup** folder. This will enable you to simply send users to **http://www.somewebsite.com/signup** to access the form.

1. In the **Files** panel, in the **signup** folder, click once on **form.html** to select it.

2. Click once more on the file name to highlight the name and allow renaming.

3. Change the file name from **form.html** to **index.html** and hit **Enter** ⟨WINDOWS⟩ or **Return** ⟨MAC⟩ to kick in the change.

4. An **Update Files** dialog will appear to ask you if you want to update your links. Hit the **Update** button. Nice!

(BROKEN LINKS)

1. If it is not already open, open the **index.html** that is on the **root** level of the website (not the one in the **signup** folder).

2. At the top of the page, in the main navbar select the **Editors' Picks** button.

3. In the **Properties** panel, change the link from **editors-pick.html** to **editorspick.html**.

   NOTE: You might be wondering why we are making a link wrong on purpose! In a moment we want to show you that Dreamweaver can catch mistakes like this.

4. Also in the navbar select the **Sign Up to Play** button.

5. In the **Properties** panel, change the link from **signup/index.html** to **sign-up/index.html.**

6. **Save** and **Close** the file.

7. Go into **Site > Check Links Sitewide**.

8. A panel will open with a list of broken links—files that Dreamweaver can't find in the local folder. It should list the two links that we just had you change. It may also list the **form** pages with broken links to **/bin/script_library/form_ handler_mail** or **/scripts/form-handler.php**. Those links are not actually bad

since the files are already on the webserver. Let's use this panel to correct the two links we know are bad. Click on the broken link name **editorspick.html** on the right to select it.

9. A folder ( ) button will appear to it's right. Click it.

10. In the dialog that appears double-click **editors-pick.html.**

11. The link will still be there, but click on the next broken link **sign-up/index.html** and the link you just fixed will disappear from the panel.

12. Click on **sign-up/index.html** so the folder ( ) button appears.

13. Click the folder ( ) button and navigate into the **signup** folder and choose **index.html.**

14. Once you are back in the **Link Checker** panel, click off of the link, into an empty area of the panel and the link will be fixed and disappear.

ORPHANED FILES

1. While you're at it, at the top left of the **Results** panel in the menu next to the word **Show,** select **Orphaned Files.**

2. Dreamweaver displays all the files with no incoming links. In this case it should just be one page named **no-links.html.** If you see other files, Dreamweaver's site cache (memory to speed up Dreamweaver) may be out of date. To fix that:
   • Go to **Site > Advanced > Recreate Site Cache.**
   • Go into **Site > Check Links Sitewide** and check the **Orphaned Files** again.

3. The **no-links.html** is an old file that we no longer need. To delete it, select the file and hit the **Delete** key. Then click **Yes** to confirm.

   NOTE: Be careful when deleting files! Just because something is listed here doesn't mean it should be deleted. Maybe someone just forgot to link to that page.

EXTERNAL LINKS

1. Lastly, in the **Link Checker** panel change the **Show** menu to **External Links.**

2. You'll see a long list of links to external URLs. You cannot test these links directly, but you can copy the URLs into a web browser and check them online. Since other sites undergo redesign and reorganization too, the page you're linking to may have been moved or deleted. The External Link Checker makes this kind of maintenance quick and easy!

Site Index. & Quick Navigation

EXERCISE PREVIEW

EXERCISE OVERVIEW

Jump menus are another type of navigation that allows you to create a long list of links from a small menu. In this case we'll make a menu of race tracks so people can look up which horses have been removed from a race (called Scratches).

1. Go to **File > Open.**

2. In the **yourname-Dreamweaver Class** folder, go into the **Public Handicapper** folder and open **jumpmenu-started.html.**

3. Go to **File > Save As.**

4. Save it into the **Public Handicapper** folder as **links.html** (replace any existing files).

ADDING A JUMP MENU

1. In the middle table, click so the cursor is blinking in the empty row beneath **Scratches** (and above **Other Links).**

2. In the **Forms** tab of the **Insert** panel, click the **Jump Menu** (🔲) button (or choose **Insert > Form > Jump Menu**).

3. The next steps will all be done in the **Insert Jump Menu** dialog. Do not hit OK until the end!

4. Next to **Text** type **Arlington Park**

5. Next to **When selected, go to URL** type **http://www.arlingtonpark.com**

6. Hit the **Plus** (⊞) button at the top to create a new menu item.

7. Next to **Text** type **Bay Meadows.**

8. Next to **When selected, go to URL** type **http://www.baymeadows.com.**

9. Hit the ⊞ at the top of the dialog again.

10. Make the text **Belmont Park**.

11. The **go to URL** should be **http://www.belmontracing.com.**

12. Toward the bottom of the dialog, next to **Options**:
    • Check **Insert go button after menu.**
    • Check **Select first item after URL change.** (This reverts the menu to its original state after you use it. This feature may not work in all browsers, such as Internet Explorer on the PC. It's still good to choose since it works in most browsers.)

13. Click **OK.**

14. On the page, you will see a menu that says **Arlington Park.** Hit **F12** (WINDOWS) or **Option–F12** (MAC) to give the jump menu a test run.

(ADDING MORE CONTENT TO THE JUMP MENU)

Adding a long list of URLs in the Jump Menu dialog can be time consuming, so let's add the content to your jump menu the fast way. We've already typed all the names and website addresses for you to copy and paste.

1. Go to **File > Open** and open **jumpmenu-done.html.**

2. In the document select the **Arlington Park** menu.

3. At the top left of the document window click the **Code** (⟨⟩Code) button.

4. There is an <option> tag for each item in the menu (indicated by the <select> tag). You've already created the first three options of the jump menu (**Arlington Park** through **Belmont Park**).

5. Highlight the option values on **line 196 through line 242** (Beulah Park through **Zia Park**).

6. Copy the code (**Ctrl–C** (WINDOWS) or **Cmd–C** (MAC)).

7. Close the file and return to **links.html**.

8. Select the **Arlington Park** jump menu on the page.

9. Switch into the **Code** (⟨⟩Code) view.

10. Place the cursor after the last closed option tag </option> (should be line 191).

11. Hit **Enter** (WINDOWS) or **Return** (MAC).

12. Press **Ctrl–V** (WINDOWS) or **Cmd–V** (MAC) to paste the code.

13. Switch back to **Design** (Design) view.

14. **Save** the file.

15. Hit **F12** (WINDOWS) or **Option–F12** (MAC) to test the full menu.

(A FINISHING TOUCH)

Since this jump menu links to external URLs, it would be best to have the links open in a new, blank browser window on top of the Public Handicapper page. You can achieve this with a small change to the target parameter in the JavaScript.

1. Select the jump menu on the page.

2. Switch into **Code** (Code) view.

3. Scroll down to the last `<option>` of the menu. Just after the `</select>` tag, you should see the following line of code:

```
<input type="button" name="go_button" id= "go_button" value="Go"
onClick="MM_jumpMenuGo('jumpMenu','parent',1)">
```

4. Change `'parent'` to `'window.open()'`. The final code should read:

```
<input type="button" name="go_button" id= "go_button" value="Go"
onClick="MM_jumpMenuGo('jumpMenu','window.open()',1)">
```

5. **Save** the file.

6. Press **F12** (WINDOWS) or **Option–F12** (MAC) to preview the new, improved navigation with links that open in new windows.

"GO" BUTTON TIP

The Insert Jump Menu dialog gives you an option for adding a go button. If you create the jump menu without a go button and decide to add one later, you'll find that the go button option has disappeared from the initial dialog. Here is how you can add a "go" button after the fact:

1. Click to the right of the Jump menu you just created.

2. Go to **Insert > Form > Button**.

3. With the button still selected, in the **Properties** panel, change the **Action** to **None**.

4. Also in the **Properties** panel next to **Value** type **Go**.

5. With the Go button still selected, go to **Window > Behaviors**.

6. In the **Behaviors** section of the **Tag Inspector** panel, click the [+] and choose **Jump Menu Go**.

7. In the dialog box that appears, just click **OK** to accept the default setting.

BONUS EXERCISES

BONUS

EXERCISE PREVIEW

EXERCISE OVERVIEW

This exercise gives you extra practice laying out a page with tables. We show you tricks to properly lay things out and create that nifty border.

1. Go into **File > New.**

2. Select the **Blank Page** tab at the left.

3. Under **Page Type** on the right select **HTML**.

4. In the **Layout** section to the right select **<none>.**

5. Click **Create.**

6. Save the file into the **Boxers Table** folder (in the **yourname-Dreamweaver Class** folder) and name it **boxer-table.html**.

Table with Rounded Corners DREAMWEAVER CS4

THE TOP SECTION OF THE PAGE

Create a table using **Insert > Table**. Put in these specs:

Rows: **1**   Columns: **3**
Table width: **500** (pixels)
Border thickness: **0**
Cell padding: **0**
Cell spacing: **0**

1. Click inside the leftmost cell and choose **Insert > Image**.

2. From the **images** folder inside the **Boxers Table** folder, choose **back_to_undies.gif**.

3. Click in the next cell (the middle one) and insert the image **boxer_prints_title.png**.

4. Click inside the rightmost cell and insert the image **more_prints.gif**.

   NOTE: The rightmost cell may be collapsed very small and hard to click into. In this case put the cursor in the middle cell and hit the **Tab** key to get to the right. Then insert the image.

5. Now we need to align these images, so click inside the first cell on the left. Make sure you don't have anything selected in it; the cursor should just be sitting in the cell. If you have trouble doing this, click on the image in the cell and then hit the **right arrow key.**

6. Now at the bottom of the **Properties** panel, set **Vert** (vertical alignment) to **Bottom**.

   NOTE: If you don't see these options in the Properties panel, you need to click the downward facing triangle in the bottom right corner to expand the panel.

7. Now click in second (middle) cell and in the **Properties** panel, set **Horz** (horizontal alignment) to **Center** and **Vert** (vertical alignment) to **Bottom**.

8. Click in third (rightmost) cell and in the **Properties** panel, set **Horz** (horizontal alignment) to **Right** and **Vert** (vertical alignment) to **Bottom**.

CREATING THE ROUND BORDER

1. So now that we've made the top section, we need to assemble the bottom section, starting with the border. **Click out in the empty area** to the right of the table, so the cursor is outside the table.

   Create a new table with these specs:

   Rows: **8**   Columns: **5**
   Table width: **500** (pixels)
   Border thickness: **0**
   Cell padding: **0**
   Cell spacing: **0**

2. Let's first create the round edged black border. Click inside the **top left** cell (of this bottom table).

3. Insert the image **corner_top_left.gif**.

4. Click in the cell at the **top right** and insert the **corner_top_right.gif** image.

5. Click in the cell at the **bottom left** and insert the **corner_bottom_left.gif**.

6. Click in the cell at the **bottom right** and insert the **corner_bottom_right.gif**.

7. Let's align these pictures in their cells. Click inside the **top left cell**. Make sure the cursor is in the cell, without the image being selected. (If you have trouble with it, click on the image and hit the right arrow key.)

8. At the bottom of the **Properties** panel, set **Vert** (vertical alignment) to **Top**. (We don't have to specify left horizontal alignment, because that is the default.)

9. Click in the **top right corner cell** (of this bottom table) and in the **Properties** panel, set **Horz** (horizontal alignment) to **Right** and **Vert** (vertical alignment) to **Top**.

10. Click in the **bottom left corner cell** and set **Vert** (vertical alignment) to **Bottom**.

11. Click in the **bottom right corner cell** and set **Horz** (horizontal alignment) to **Right** and **Vert** (vertical alignment) to **Bottom**.

12. Now that the corners are all in place, we can see that the left and right columns aren't tight to the size of the images in them... they are too big, so we'll need to specify an exact width.

13. Click in the top left corner cell and in the bottom half of the Properties panel you'll notice the cell options. Enter in **W** (Width): **31** and **H** (Height): **30**.

14. Click in the top right corner cell and again, in Properties panel, enter in **W** (Width): **31** and **H** (Height): **30**.

    That's looking better. Now we need to connect these corners with a line. We'll do this by taking a small black box and stretching it to form a line between the end images.

15. If you look in the first row of this table we're working with, you'll notice there are three cells in between the corner images, so you'll need to merge them into one. To do this, click and drag across the cells you want to merge, as shown below:

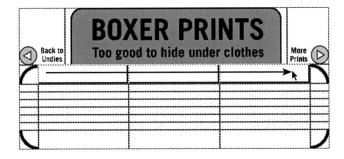

16. Click the **Merge Cells** (▣) button on the lower left of the **Properties** panel.

17. Click in this new cell and insert the **black_box.gif** image.

    With the image still selected, in the **Properties** panel change the **W** to **438**.

18. The line doesn't match up with the corners though. To fix this, our cursor needs to be in the cell, but since the image is the whole width of the cell we can't just click in it. The trick is to click on the image, and then hit the **right arrow key** on the keyboard.

19. Now at the bottom of the **Properties** panel you should see the cell options. Change the **Vert** (Vertical Alignment) to **top**. Voilà!

20. Let's do the same thing at the bottom. Select the cells between the corner images as you did previously.

21. Click the **Merge Cells** (▣) button in the **Properties** panel.

22. Click in this new cell and insert the **black_box.gif** image.

23. With the image still selected, in the **Properties** panel make: **W: 438**

24. To match up the line with the corners, click on the image, and then hit the **right arrow key** on the keyboard.

25. Now at the bottom of the **Properties** panel you should see the cell options. Change the **Vert** (vertical alignment) to **bottom**.

26. Now for the left side of the border, click and drag down the cells you want to merge as shown below:

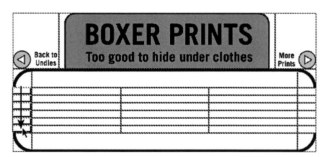

27. Click the **Merge Cells** (▣) button in the Properties panel.

28. Click in this new cell and insert the **black_box.gif** image.

    With the image still selected, in the **Properties** panel make: **H: 615**

29. The line should already match up with the corners, cool!

30. Now for the right side of the border, select the cells between the corner images as you did just a few steps ago.

31. Click the **Merge Cells** (▣) button on the lower left of the Properties panel.

32. Click in this new cell and insert the **black_box.gif** image.

    With the image still selected, in the **Properties** panel make: **H: 615**

33. To match up the line with the corners, click in that cell and in the **Properties** panel change the **Horz** (horizontal alignment) to **right**.

LAYING OUT THE BOXER SHORTS CONTENT

Now we need to lay out all the boxer shorts with their name, price and order buttons.

1. Looking at the border, the second cell in the second row is the first "empty" cell. Click inside that cell and insert the **boxers-army.jpg**.

2. Wow, most likely the rest of the table cells will have collapsed to the right hand side, but you still need to put images there. To get around this, we'll use the Tab key to tab into them. With the Army boxers image still selected hit the **Tab** key **twice**.

3. Now insert the **boxers-tropical.jpg**.

4. Now inserting the images will be easier. Go ahead and insert the rest of the images using the diagram below as a guide to what goes where:

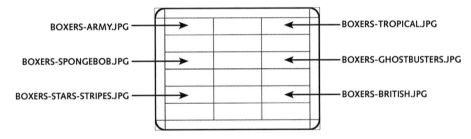

5. **Save** the document.

6. To center the images, select the left boxer image cells by clicking in and dragging from an empty area in the **top left** cell to the **bottom left** "empty" cell. (Be careful NOT to click on the image, but rather click inside the cell, outside the image.)

7. In the **Properties** panel now change the **Horz** (horizontal alignment) to **center**.

8. Now center the right boxer images. Click in and drag from an empty area in the **top right** cell to the **bottom right** "empty" cell. (Be careful NOT to click on the image, but rather click inside the cell, outside the image.)

9. In the **Properties** panel now change the **Horz** (horizontal alignment) to **center**.

10. Now for the captions. Click in the cell under the Army boxers image (on the top left).

11. Type in **Camouflage - $15.00**.

12. Hit **Shift–Enter** (WINDOWS) or **Shift–Return** (MAC).

13. Insert the image **add_to_cart.gif**.

14. With the Add to Cart image still selected, in the **Properties** panel, give a **V space** of **4**.

15. Copy everything in that cell.

16. Paste it in the cell below each of the other boxers.

17. Then change the captions to:

Image:	Caption you need to type in:
Tropical boxers (on the top right)	**Tropical - $15.00**
SpongeBob boxers (on the middle left)	**SpongeBob - $15.00**
Ghost Busters boxers (on the middle right)	**Ghost Busters - $15.00**
Stars and Stripes boxers (on the bottom left)	**Stars and Stripes - $15.00**
British flag boxers (on the bottom right)	**British - $15.00**

18. The bottoms of the captions are too close to the boxers below, so let's change the height of the cells. Click in the caption cell for the Army boxers. In the **Properties** panel under **H** (height) type in **65**.

19. Give the caption cell for the **Tropical boxers** a height of **65**.

20. Give the caption cells for the **SpongeBob** and **Ghost Busters** boxers a height of **65**.

21. Hit **F12** (WINDOWS) or **Option–F12** (MAC) to preview.

22. The last thing to do it to align the captions to the top of their cells. Click in the caption underneath the Army boxers. In the **Properties** panel change the **Vert** (vertical alignment) to **Top**.

23. Repeat the last step for all the captions.

> **WRAPPING THINGS UP**

1. Now that's starting to look like a good page! But we still have some finishing up. First of all, we need some space between the two columns of boxers.

2. Let's adjust the space in that middle column. Click in the top cell of that column.

NOTE: If you can't get your cursor easily into the narrow cell, click on the Army boxers image to the left and hit the **Tab** key.

3. In the **Properties** panel under **W** (width) type in **20**.

4. **Preview** the page. It probably looks great, but in some older browsers it may not display correctly with the blank table cell. In order to make sure it works right in all browsers, we'll use a common web designer's trick.

5. Click inside the top cell in that middle column and insert the image **spacer.gif**. With the image still selected, in the Properties panel change the W (Width) to **20**.

Some browsers don't recognize the size of a table cell regardless of its specified width. By using this invisible, transparent, spacer image as a "shim" a browser is forced to display the correct space because tables can't shrink an image.

6. The two navigation buttons on the top of the page are a little close the to the line, so select the **Back to Undies** graphic. In the **Properties** panel make: **V Space: 10**

7. Select the **More Prints** image on the right and set **V Space: 10**

8. Select the heading image at the top and set the **Alt** to **Boxer Prints - Too good to hide under clothes**.

9. Add the following **Alt** attribute descriptions to their appropriate boxer short images (this can be found in the **Properties** panel).

   Camouflage Boxers   **Tropical Boxers**
   SpongeBob Boxers   **Ghost Busters Boxers**
   Stars and Stripes Boxers   **British Boxers**

10. Now give all the Add to cart images an alt of **Add to Cart**. (NOTE: Once you give the first image that alt, to do the same thing to the others, you can select an image and then press **Ctrl–Y** (WINDOWS) or **Cmd–Y** (MAC) to repeat that. Then select the next image and press **Ctrl–Y** (WINDOWS) or **Cmd–Y** (MAC) again.)

    According to W3C specifications (see sidebar to the right) all images need an alt attribute. Visually impaired people that have web pages read to them probably don't need to know about the border images. In this case we insert an **empty** alt attribute. That way we adhere to web standards and still keep a good user experience.

11. To add alt attributes to the border images, select each one of the 4 corners and 4 sides and in the **Properties** panel. Then next to **Alt**, click the menu button and select **<empty>** for each of these images.

12. Let's center everything on the page. Click inside the top table.

13. From the **Quick Tag Selector** in the bottom left corner of the document, click the **<table>** tag to select the table.

14. In the **Properties** panel change **Align** to **Center**.

15. Align the bottom table this way as well.

16. Finally, in the Toolbar at the top of the window, next to **Title:** make the title of the page **Boxer Prints - Too Good to Hide Under Clothes**.

17. **Save** and hit **F12** (WINDOWS) or **Option–F12** (MAC) to preview. Congrats, you're on the way to being a table wiz!

WHAT IS THE W3C?

The W3C (World Wide Web Consortium) is the organization that decides current and future web standards. The idea of web standards is that if all browsers render webpages according to W3C specs, all browsers would render the same, so you wouldn't have to worry about coding for different browsers. You can learn more about them at http://www.w3.org.

Not search engine friendly!
Good for personal pages

EXERCISE PREVIEW

EXERCISE OVERVIEW

Frames can be tricky to create, but we make it easy for you in this exercise. You'll create the frames and link the pages for an entire frames-based site.

ROUGHING OUT THE FRAMESET

1. In Dreamweaver, go into **File > New.**

2. In the **Blank Page** tab at the left, choose Page Type: **HTML,** Layout: **<none>** and click **Create.**

3. This will be a framed document, so you need to do two things. First, go into **View > Visual Aids > Frame Borders.** This will give you an extra border around the edge of the document window.

   NOTE: You can also show the frame borders as shown below by clicking the Visual Aids button in the Toolbar and choosing Frame Borders.

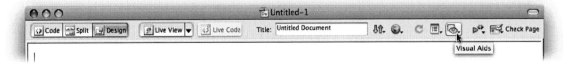

4. Make sure the **Rulers** are showing **(View > Rulers > Show).**

5. To divide the page into two columns (frames), put your cursor over the left border of the page. You will see a double-arrow (⟷) indicating that you can proceed. Drag the border to the right about 200 pixels.

6. We want to add a row to the top that stretches all the way across. To do this, move the cursor over the top border but this time hold **Ctrl** ⟨WINDOWS⟩ or **Command** ⟨MAC⟩ while you drag. This ensures that the row will stretch all the way across, rather than create a row of two columns.

7. You should now have three frames. See the figure at right to make sure you have set it up right.

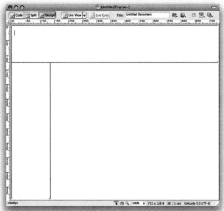

8. Let's save this Frameset. Do a **File > Save Frameset As,** save it into the **Frames Site** folder as **index.html.** If you don't see **Save Frameset As,** click one of the grey frame borders to select it.

9. Click inside the **top** frame.

10. Go into **File > Open in Frame** and from the **Frames Site** folder open **top.html.**

11. Click inside the **left** frame.

12. Go into **File > Open in Frame** and choose **nav.html.**

13. Click inside the **right** frame.

14. Go into **File > Open in Frame** and choose **index-content.html.**

15. To be safe, do a **File > Save All.**

16. **Preview** the file. Resize the window and notice how all the frames change proportionally. This doesn't work very well visually. Switch back to Dreamweaver.

(**FINISHING UP THE FRAMESET**)

1. Open the **Frames** panel **(Window > Frames).**

2. As shown below, in the **Frames** panel you can see a thumbnail of each frame. Click on the **top** frame to select it.

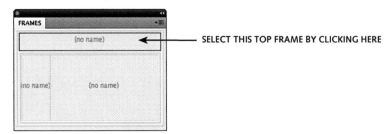

SELECT THIS TOP FRAME BY CLICKING HERE

3. As shown below, in the **Properties** panel, name this frame **header.**

ENTER THE NAME "HEADER" HERE

Also in the **Properties** panel set:
- Scroll: **No**
- Margin width: **0**
- Margin height: **0**

4. In the **Frames** panel click on the **left** frame and in the **Properties** panel:
   - Frame name: **nav**
   - Scrolling: **No**
   - Margin width: **0**
   - Margin height: **0**

5. In the **Frames** panel click on the **right** frame.

6. In the **Properties** panel name it **content.**

7. OK, here it gets slightly tricky. In order to select the outermost frameset, instead of an individual frame, click on the outermost outline in the **Frames** panel (shown below). It's the one that goes around every frame.

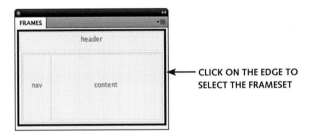

CLICK ON THE EDGE TO
SELECT THE FRAMESET

8. As shown below, on the right of the **Properties** panel you will see an icon designating the two rows in the master frameset.

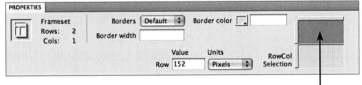

CLICK HERE TO SELECT THE TOP ROW

Click on the **top** row and set:
Borders: **No**
Border width: **0**
Row Value: **139 pixels**

9. Still in the **Properties** panel click on the bottom row icon and:

   Leave the Value, but under **Units** change Pixels to **Relative** (this makes the bottom row variable for users with different size screens/windows).

10. While we have the frameset selected, let's give this page a title.
    In the Toolbar at the top of the page, next to **Title:** type in **Diane's Travels.**

EXERCISE

11. As shown below, to select the nested frameset, click on the outline in the **Frames** panel that only goes around the bottom two frames.

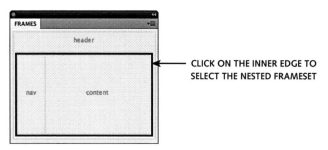

CLICK ON THE INNER EDGE TO
SELECT THE NESTED FRAMESET

12. In **Properties**, you see the frames icon with columns instead of rows. Click on the **left** column and set:
    Borders: **No**
    Border width: **0**
    Column Value: **200 pixels.**

13. Still in the **Properties** panel, click on the **right** frame in the thumbnail and change the Column Value from **Pixels** to **Relative.**

14. Do a **File > Save All.**

15. **Preview** the page in a browser and try clicking on one of the navbar links on the left. You see that they link to pages, but the pages show up in the same left-hand frame. We want the links to come up in the right frame, so we must target them.

16. Switch back to Dreamweaver.

(LINKING WITHIN A FRAMESET)

1. Click on **Travel Packages** button graphic in the **nav** frame.

2. In the **Properties** panel, next to **Target** click on the menu (⬍) and select **content** (or you can just type **content** in the **Target** field).

3. Do the same thing to the rest of the navbar graphics (Destination Info, Trip Planning, About Us, and Contact). Target them to the **content** frame by selecting it from the **Target** menu (⬍). Or better yet, just select the navbar graphic and press **Ctrl–Y** (WINDOWS) or **Command–Y** (MAC) to repeat the target you just did! For each remaining graphic just select it and press **Ctrl–Y** (WINDOWS) or **Command–Y** (MAC).

4. Do a **Save All,** then **Preview** your handiwork!

(ALTERNATE METHODS)

Please note that there are multiple ways to build framesets.
For instance you can use the presets in the **Insert** panel. To see them:

• Create a new document.
• In the **Insert** panel, click on the **Layout** tab.
• Click the **Frames** (▤) button and from the menu choose the correct one.

You can also do something very similar by doing a **File > New**, choosing
Page from Sample on the left and then **Frameset**. You can then choose the
appropriate layout on the right.

EXERCISE PREVIEW

EXERCISE OVERVIEW

Quicktime may no longer be as popular as Flash when it comes to putting video on the web, but it is still a great option for high quality video. It can be a bit tricky to add it properly to a web page, so in this exercise we show the professional way that works on all browsers.

DEFINING A SITE

1. When inserting a movie, Dreamweaver will generate JavaScript files needed to display it. These files are best put into a folder on the root level of our site, so we should define a site. We'll be using the Woofing Cookies site we worked on earlier. You may still have that site defined. To check, go to **Site > Manage Sites.**

2. If you have a site named **yourname-Woofing Cookies,** select it in the list and click **Done.** Skip the following sidebar. If you do not have a site named **yourname-Woofing Cookies,** click **Done** and do the following sidebar.

IF YOU DO NOT HAVE A WOOFING COOKIES SITE DEFINED

1. In Dreamweaver, go to **Site > New Site.**

2. A **Site Definition** dialog will open. Click the **Advanced** tab at the top.

3. For **Site name** enter **yourname-Woofing Cookies.**

4. Next to **Local root folder,** click on the folder (📁) icon and navigate until you get to **Class Files.** Go into the **yourname-Dreamweaver Class** folder and

   WINDOWS: Double-click on the subfolder **Woofing Cookies.**
   Then click the **Select** button. Click **OK** to finish defining the site.

   MAC: Select the **Woofing Cookies** folder and click **Choose.**
   Click **OK** to finish defining the site.

ADDING THE MOVIE TO A PAGE

1. In the **Files** panel double-click **interview-video.html** to open it.

2. Click in the empty layer below the **Reunion Tour** graphic.
   (The layer just looks like a empty box with a grey border.)

3. Go to **Insert > Media > ActiveX.**

4. An **ActiveX icon** 🎛 will appear on the page.

5. In the **Properties** panel at the bottom of the screen, notice that both **Width (W)** and **Height (H)** are 32. Our movie is bigger than this, so we'll make room for it.

6. Change the **W** to **310.** Change the **H** to **249.**

   NOTE: The movie is actually **233** pixels tall. Adding **16 pixels** to the movie's **height** makes space for the **player controls** to be seen and used at the bottom of the movie.

7. In the **Properties** panel, check **Embed.**

8. Next to **Src,** click the Browse folder (📁) icon.

9. In the dialog that appears, click the **Site Root** button.

10. Go into the **videos** folder and choose **studio-interview.mov.** If you don't see the file, set the **Files of type** menu to **All Files (*)** and then you should be able to see it. Hit **OK.**

11. Go to **File > Open.**

12. In the **Woofing Cookies** folder open the file **quicktime.txt.**

13. Copy **clsid:02BF25D5-8C17-4B23-BC80-D3488ABDDC6B.**

14. Go back into **interview-video.html.**

15. In the **Properties** panel, in the **ClassID** field, **Paste** the ClassID you just copied and hit **Return** to make the change.

16. If previewing in Internet Explorer, choose **Commands > Insert Mark of the Web.** This will let you preview without having to deal with the yellow alert bar.

17. Press **F12** (WINDOWS) or **Option–F12** (MAC) to preview. Dreamweaver will popup an alert explaining that it has created some JavaScript files that will need to be uploaded to the webserver. If you get that message just click OK.

ADDING MOVIE PARAMETERS

1. Not bad! But what if you don't want the movie to start playing automatically? By adding a simple command to the existing code, the viewer can then decide when they want the movie to start once on the page.

2. Click on the **ActiveX movie.**

3. In the **Properties** panel, click the **Parameters** button.
   • Under parameter, type **autostart.**
   • Under value, type **false.**
   Click **OK.**

4. **Preview** again and you will see the movie does not start automatically.

5. There are a few more parameters to add for best practices.
   Back in Dreamweaver, click the **Parameters** button again.

6. Click the **Plus** (✚) button to add more parameters.
   • Under parameter, type **codebase.**
   • Under value, type **http://www.apple.com/qtactivex/qtplugin.cab**
     If the user does not already have the ActiveX control installed on his or
     her system, the **codebase** parameter tells the browser where to find it
     for downloading.
   • Under parameter, type **pluginspage.**
   • Under value, type **http://www.apple.com/quicktime/**
     Similarly, the **pluginspage** parameter tells the browser where to find the
     Quicktime plugin for downloading, if not already installed.
   Click **OK.**

7. When putting this online, you have to upload the **.html** file, the **.mov** file, and
   the **Scripts** folder that Dreamweaver created.

REFERENCE MATERIAL

REFERENCE

Once you create your site, you will want to be listed on the major Web search engines. There are two types of listings: free and paid. Unfortunately, these days you really will need to pay to get listed in most places. However it is possible with the use of strategic keywords that you can show up on Google or Yahoo for free.

Before submitting your site to various engines/directories, you need to do a few things to the important pages on your site (those that you would like to be indexed, or "found" by the search engines).

PAGE TITLES

Google will index the title of your pages and use those words as priority indexed words. In this case, the more information your title has, the better. For example, the title of your apple-picking farm might be **Cornwall Farms.** But that does not mean anything to people who search the internet for **apple picking.**

What works better is this: **Apple Picking In New York State.**

Try to make your titles as descriptive as possible, but try to keep them 60 characters or less. Difficult, yes, but that's the hand we have been dealt!

META TAGS

META tags go within the HEAD tag to provide information on your page. There are a variety of META tags but the most important is the "description" tag. The description tag is what a search engine will usually display as the summary of your site. Another popular meta tag is the "keyword" tag. Unfortunately, it's virtually irrelevant now. Only Yahoo uses it at all, and even then, hardly. The best thing to do is create a keyword tag, just in case it IS ever used, and copy the description tag into it. For more information on strategy to follow for better listings, check out **www.searchenginewatch.com.**

META TAG SYNTAX

Here is an example of how the Meta tags might look for an apple-picking site:

```
<HEAD>
<TITLE>Apple Picking in New York State</TITLE>
<META name="description" content="Cornwall Farms Apple Picking in Upstate New York State">
<META name="keywords" content="Cornwall Farms Apple Picking in Upstate New York State">
</HEAD>
```

When a surfer does a search, the site will usually show up in this context:

Apple Picking in New York State
Cornwall Farms Apple Picking in Upstate New York State.

THE SUBMISSION PROCESS FOR FREE LISTINGS

First, you have to submit the pages you want indexed to Google and Yahoo. This is simple. Compile a list of URLs that you want coming up as searches. In Noble Desktop's case, we would want, for example, our Dreamweaver and Flash class pages to show up. Once you have a list of pages to submit, follow these steps:

1. Go to **google.com.**

2. Click on **About Google** (bottom of homepage).

3. Click on **Submit your content to Google.**

4. Click on **Add your URL to Google's index.**

5. Submit the URLs!

6. OK, now go to **Yahoo.**

7. Click on **Suggest a Site** (bottom of page).

8. Click on **Submit Your Site for Free.**

9. Submit all the URLs!

10. Finally, go to **dmoz.org,** which is the Open Directory. There you can submit your site for inclusion in their directory. This directory is becoming more irrelevant, but it can't hurt. Of course, if you are pressed for time, you could skip this one.

PAID PLACEMENT

The three big guns in paid search are Google, Yahoo, and MSN. Google is the easiest and most popular. Nearly 70% of all web searches are done through Google and that is still growing. You may be amazed at the traffic that will immediately flow to your site after putting up a pay-per-click ad.

GOOGLE

To begin placing ads on Google right now, just go to google.com and click on Advertising Programs. There are two options: AdWords and AdSense. AdWords is Google's pay-per-click program that shows your ads and only costs if someone clicks on your ad. AdSense is used for running other people's ads on your website. To advertise your site to the world right away, click on AdWords. We don't recommend running Google ads on your own site, though some people do profit from that.

YAHOO

Yahoo still gets a fair amount of search, although their share is declining. You can list your site in two ways with Yahoo: through a paid directory listing, and through pay-per-click advertising. The pay-per-click advertising works the same as on Google. Definitely save all of your search descriptions from Google in a text file, and use them to submit to Yahoo as well. The Yahoo directory listing costs $299 per year, and frankly, we don't see any benefit to it. Our "free" listings show up before the directory listing, so we would skip this part of it.

MSN

Microsoft used to share its pay-per-click ad revenue with Overture, which was bought by Yahoo. Then it launched its own in-house brand, Microsoft Ad Sense. We haven't used it, as we rarely got traffic from MSN. However it is worth trying out your ads there as well. You can always stop your ad campaigns any time. There is no negative to giving them a spin and seeing if you get traffic.

FOR MORE INFORMATION

Be sure to check **searchenginewatch.com** for details on each submission process. They give you all kinds of up-to-date information and strategies for Search Engine Optimization. Good luck!

If you have an HTML page that you want to convert to XHTML, here's an easy way.

1. Open the HTML file.

2. Go to **Modify > Page Properties.**

3. On the left, click **Title/Encoding.**

4. Change Document Type (DTD) to **XHTML 1.0 Transitional** (or the Strict depending on your preference).

5. Click **OK.**

6. You may get a warning about empty Alt tags, just click **OK.**

DIFFERENCES BETWEEN HTML AND XHTML

There are just a few subtle differences between HTML and XHTML. Asides for a different DOCTYPE, here are the few differences.

In HTML some tags have no ending tag. But in XHTML everything must either have an ending tag, or be "self-ending" tags.
For example:

HTML: `<br>`
XHTML: `<br />`

HTML: `<img src="image.jpg">`
XHTML: `<img src="image.jpg" />`

In HTML tags can be uppercase or lowercase, but in In XHTML, everything must be lowercase. For example:

HTML: `<TABLE>`
XHTML: `<table>`

Windows has a free FTP feature built right into to Windows Explorer
(the Desktop file browser).

UPLOADING WEBPAGES TO A REMOTE WEBSERVER USING WINDOWS EXPLORER

Before proceeding, make sure you have done these things:

– Created a homepage that is called **index.html.**
– Assembled all of the documents you need to upload in one
  easy-to-access folder.
– Named all your files with lowercase letters.
– Given all HTML documents a **.html** extension.
– Given all graphics files either **.gif** or **.jpg** extensions.
– Have the connection information given to you by your webhost.

1. **Double-click My Computer,** or press **Windows–E** to open Windows Explorer.

2. In the **Address** bar type **ftp://your ftp address** and press **Enter.** On Windows
   Vista the Address bar is not labelled, but it's the top field next to the back and
   forward arrows.

3. When asked, enter the appropriate info as it was given to you by your host:

   User name: **yourusername**
   Password: **yourpassword**

   Click **Log On.**

4. You should see a window containing files, exactly like the Windows Explorer
   that you are used to using to browse local files. These are the remote server files
   for your site (if this is your first time uploading, there may only be 1 or 2 files).
   You may still need to go into a specific directory (for example **www**) as directed
   by our webhost. **Double-click** on the appropriate directory to get into it.

5. Go to **View > Details** (on Windows Vista use the **Views** button).

6. You are now ready to upload your files. In order to do this move the Explorer
   window to the right side of the monitor.

7. Press **Windows–E** to open a new Explorer window and go into your computer,
   and navigate to the folder where your local website files are stored.

8. Go to **View > Details.**

9. Arrange the two windows so you see your local files on the left and the remote
   server files on the right.
   TIP: If these are the only 2 windows open, you can **Right-click** the taskbar and
        choose **Tile Windows Vertically** (XP) or **Show Windows Side by Side** (Vista)
        to do this quickly.

10. To upload a file, simply drag a file from your computer's window on the left to the remote server window on the right. If you want to upload more than one file, **Control-click** on each file and then drag them all over. Additionally, if you click on one file and **Shift-click** another file, all the files in between them will also be selected.

    If you get confused as to which window is the FTP server, just look in the **Address** bar for the ftp:// address.

11. Once you have uploaded everything, start a web browser, and check out your new or updated site!

Cyberduck is a great, free FTP program for the Mac.

UPLOADING WEBPAGES TO A REMOTE WEBSERVER USING CYBERDUCK

Before proceeding, make sure you have done these things:
– You have downloaded and installed **Cyberduck** from **http://www.cyberduck.ch**
– Created a homepage that is called **index.html.**
– Assembled all of the documents you need to upload in one easy-to-access folder.
– Named all your files with **lowercase** letters.
– Given all HTML documents a **.html** extension.
– Given all graphics files either **.gif, .jpg, or .png** extensions.
– Have the connection information given to you by your webhost.

1. Launch **Cyberduck.**

2. Click the **Open Connection** button at the top left of the main window.

3. Then enter this information:
   Server: **your ftp address**
   Username: **yourusername**
   Password: **yourpassword**
   Under the **More Options** section:
   Path: enter one if provided by your host (not everyone has this).
       Typically **www** or **public_html**

4. To connect to the server, click **Connect.**
   TIP: Once connected you can choose **Bookmark > New Bookmark** to save all this information for future use.

5. Once connected you will see the window that lists the files for your site (if this is your first time uploading, there may only be 1 or 2 files/folders). If they aren't there, you may still need to go into the right directory. Double-click on the directory to get into it.

6. You are now ready to upload your files. In order to do this move the Cyberduck window to the side so you can see your desktop and it at the same time.

7. Go into your computer and navigate to the folder where your website files are stored. Arrange this window and the Cyberduck window so they are side by side. You should now be able to see your local files and the remote website files (in Cyberduck) at the same time.

8. To upload a file, simply drag a file from your computer's window onto the Cyberduck window. If you want to upload more than one file **Command–click** on each file and then drag them all over to the Cyberduck window. Additionally, if you click on one file and **Shift-click** another file, all the files in between them will also be selected.

9. A transfer window will appear, showing the progress of the upload. You can close it if you wish.

10. Once you have uploaded everything, start your web browser, and check out your new or updated website!

THIS IS A FAVICON (A FAVORITES ICON)

As shown above, some websites have a small icon next to their URL. This is called a Favicon, short for favorites icon. It got its name when Internet Explorer (PC) put this icon next to a website that is saved as a favorite. From then on, the Favicon shows up whenever the site is viewed. Other browsers (Safari, Firefox, etc.) have since started showing Favicons all the time, even if the site isn't a favorite. Windows IE still won't show the icon unless it's a favorite.

Favicon images are saved in a Windows Icon format (.ico) which Photoshop can only open and save if you get a free plug-in. Even though it's called a Windows Icon it works on a Mac.

1. Go to **http://www.telegraphics.com.au/sw/** and download the **ICO (Windows Icon) file format** plug-in for Photoshop.

2. As the included directions say, you install the plug-in by copying the **icoformat** file into: **C: Drive > Program Files > Adobe > Adobe Photoshop CS4 > Plug-Ins > File Formats** folder (WINDOWS) or **Hard Drive > Applications > Adobe Photoshop CS4 > Plug-Ins > File Formats** folder (MAC).

3. Restart Photoshop if it was running.

4. In Photoshop create an image that is:
   • 16 pixels wide by 16 pixels tall
   • RGB
   • 72 ppi
   • 8 bit

5. Make the icon look however you want.

6. Go to **File > Save As** and:
   • Under Format choose **ICO (Windows Icon)**
   • Name it **favicon.ico**
   • Save it into the root folder of the website.
   • After saving you will be asked to choose a format. Choose **Standard ICO.**

7. Upload the **favicon.ico** file to the root folder of your website.

   That's it! Check out your website to see the new favicon.

NOTE: If you're on a Mac using Safari you'll need to force Safari to get the latest icons by trashing it's icon cache folder. To do this:

1. Go into **Hard Drive > Users > yourusername > Library > Safari.**

2. Trash the **Icon** folder that is there.

3. Restart Safari if it was running.

Now Safari will show the latest website icons.

INSERT

Non-Breaking Space ( )	Ctrl-Shift-Space
Line Break 	Shift-Return
Image	Ctrl-Alt-I
Table	Ctrl-Alt-T

MODIFY

Quick Tag Editor	Ctrl-T
Show Code Navigator	Ctrl-Alt-Click

WORKING WITH TABLES

Select individual (or multiple, discontinuous) table cells	Ctrl-click cell(s)
Select Table (with cursor inside the table)	Ctrl-A (may need to do twice)
Insert Row	Ctrl-M
Insert Column	Ctrl-Shift-A
Delete Row	Ctrl-Shift-M
Delete Column	Ctrl-Shift-hyphen(-)
Merge Selected Cells	Ctrl-Alt-M
Split Cell...	Ctrl-Alt-S
Increase Column Span	Ctrl-Shift-]
Decrease Column Span	Ctrl-Shift-[
Add new row at bottom of table	with cursor in bottom right table cell, hit Tab

WORKING WITH FRAMES

Add a new frame to frameset	In the Frames panel select the frame, then in your document window Alt-drag frame border
Pull out solid frame (creates Nested Frameset)	Ctrl-drag frame border
Select a frame	Alt-click in frame
Select next frame or frameset	Alt-Right arrow
Select previous frame or frameset	Alt-Left arrow
Select parent frameset	Alt-Up arrow
Select first child frame or frameset	Alt-Down arrow

WORKING WITH IMAGES

Replace image with a different one	Double-click image
Edit image in external editor	Ctrl-Double-click image

WORKING WITH LAYERS

Select a layer (without having to click its grab tag)	Ctrl-Shift-click

WORKING WITH LINKS

Make Link	Ctrl-L
Remove Link	Ctrl-Shift-L
Open the link-to document in Dreamweaver	Ctrl-Double-click link
Drag & drop to create link	Select the text, then Shift-drag it to file in Site panel

FORMATTING TEXT

None	Ctrl-0
Heading 1	Ctrl-1
Heading 2	Ctrl-2
Heading 3	Ctrl-3
Heading 4	Ctrl-4
Heading 5	Ctrl-5
Heading 6	Ctrl-6
Paragraph	Ctrl-Shift-P
Left	Ctrl-Alt-Shift-L
Center	Ctrl-Alt-Shift-C
Right	Ctrl-Alt-Shift-R
Justify	Ctrl-Alt-Shift-J
Text Indent	Ctrl-Alt+]
Text Outdent	Ctrl-Alt+[

DOCUMENT EDITING

Go to Next Word	Ctrl-Right arrow
Go to Previous Word	Ctrl-Left arrow
Go to Previous Paragraph	Ctrl-Up arrow
Go to Next Paragraph	Ctrl-Down arrow
Select Until Next Word	Ctrl-Shift-Right arrow
Select From Previous Word	Ctrl-Shift-Left arrow
Select From Previous Paragraph	Ctrl-Shift-Up arrow
Select Until Next Paragraph	Ctrl-Shift-Down arrow
Edit Tag	Shift-F5
Exit Paragraph	Ctrl-Enter

CODE EDITING

Show Code Hints	Ctrl-Space
Select Parent Tag	Ctrl-[
Select Child	Ctrl-]
Balance Braces	Ctrl-'
Find Next (Find Again)	F3
Select line up/down	Shift-Up/Down arrow
Character select left/right	Shift-Left/Right arrow
Select to page up/down	Shift-Page Up/Page Down
Move to word on left/right	Ctrl-Left/Right arrow
Select to word on left/right	Ctrl-Shift-Left/Right arrow
Move to start/end of line	Home/ End
Select to start/end of line	Shift-Home/End
Move to top/end of file	Ctrl-Home/End
Select to start/end of file	Ctrl-Shift-Home/End
Go to Line	Ctrl-G
Indent Code	Ctrl-Shift->
Outdent Code	Ctrl-Shift-<

VIEW

Switch between Code and Design Views	Ctrl-`
Refresh Design View	F5
Live View	Alt-F11

WORKING WITH DOCUMENTS & PANELS

Show/Hide Panels	F4
Switch to Next Document	Ctrl-Tab
Switch to Previous Document	Ctrl-Shift-Tab
Assets	F11
Behaviors	Shift-F4
Bindings	Ctrl-F10
Code Inspector	F10
Components	Ctrl-F7
CSS Styles	Shift-F11
Databases	Ctrl-Shift-F10
Files	F8
Frames	Shift-F2
History	Shift-F10
AP Elements (Layers)	F2
Properties	Ctrl-F3
Reference	Shift-F1
Results	F7
Server Behaviors	Ctrl-F9
Snippets	Shift-F9
Tag Inspector	F9

MISC

Check Spelling	Shift-F7
Get File from Server	Ctrl-Shift-D
Put File on Server	Ctrl-Shift-U

⬈ NOBLE DESKTOP

<!--Exceptional computer graphics training.-->

594 Broadway, Suite 1202, New York, NY 10012
212.226.4149 www.nobledesktop.com

Dreamweaver CS4

Useful Keyboard Shortcuts—Mac

www.nobledesktop.com

INSERT

Non-Breaking Space ( )......⌘-Shift-Space (works in Code & Design views)
Option-Space also works, but only in Design view
Line Break <br>.. Shift-Return
Image ....⌘-Opt-I
Table ....⌘-Opt-T

MODIFY

Quick Tag Editor ....⌘-T
Show Code Navigator ....⌘-Opt-Click

WORKING WITH TABLES

Select individual (or multiple, discontinuous) table cells................⌘-click cell(s)
Select Table (with cursor inside the table)................⌘-A (may need to do twice)
Insert Row ....⌘-M
Insert Column ....⌘-Shift-A
Delete Row ....⌘-Shift-M
Delete Column ....⌘-Shift-hyphen(-)
Merge Selected Cells..⌘-Opt-M
Split Cell...⌘-Opt-S
Increase Column Span ....⌘-Shift-]
Decrease Column Span ....⌘-Shift-[
Add new row at bottom of table ....with cursor in bottom right table cell, hit Tab

WORKING WITH FRAMES

Add a new frame to frameset....................In the Frames panel select the frame,
then in your document window Opt-drag frame border
Pull out solid frame (creates Nested Frameset)...................⌘-drag frame border
Select a frame...Shift-Opt-click in frame
Select next frame or frameset ....⌘-Right arrow
Select previous frame or frameset.........................⌘-Left arrow
Select parent frameset ....⌘-Up arrow
Select first child frame or frameset ....⌘-Down arrow

WORKING WITH IMAGES

Replace image with a different one........................Double-click image
Edit image in external editor ....⌘-Double-click image

WORKING WITH LAYERS

Select a layer (without having to click its grab tag) ....⌘-Shift-click

WORKING WITH LINKS

Make Link..⌘-L
Remove Link..⌘-Shift-L
Open the link-to document in Dreamweaver ....⌘-Double-click link
Drag & drop to create link ....Select the text, then Shift-drag it to file in Files panel

FORMATTING TEXT

None ....⌘-0
Heading 1..⌘-1
Heading 2..⌘-2
Heading 3..⌘-3
Heading 4..⌘-4
Heading 5..⌘-5
Heading 6..⌘-6
Paragraph..⌘-Shift-P
Left..⌘-Opt-Shift-L
Center..⌘-Opt-Shift-C
Right...⌘-Opt-Shift-R
Justify..⌘-Opt-Shift-J
Text Indent...⌘-Opt+]
Text Outdent ....⌘-Opt+[

DOCUMENT EDITING

Go to Next Word..⌘-Right arrow
Go to Previous Word...⌘-Left arrow
Go to Previous Paragraph..⌘-Up arrow
Go to Next Paragraph..⌘-Down arrow
Select Until Next Word ....⌘-Shift-Right arrow
Select From Previous Word ....⌘-Shift-Left arrow
Select From Previous Paragraph........................⌘-Shift-Up arrow
Select Until Next Paragraph ....⌘-Shift-Down arrow
Edit Tag Shift-F5
Exit Paragraph ....⌘-Return

CODE EDITING

Show Code Hints.. Control-Space
Quick Tag Editor..⌘-T
Select Parent Tag...⌘-[
Select Child...⌘-]
Balance Braces..⌘-'
Find Next (Find Again) ....⌘-G
Select line up/down...Shift-Up/Down arrow
Character select left/right.......................................Shift-Left/Right arrow
Select to page up/down.....................................Shift-Page Up/Page Down
Move to word on left/right.................................⌘-Left/Right arrow
Select to word on left/right.................................⌘-Shift-Left/Right arrow
Move to start/end of line ....Home/ End
Select to start/end of line ....Shift-Home/End
Move to top/end of file...⌘-Home/End
Select to start/end of file ....⌘-Shift-Home/End
Go to Line ....⌘-,
Indent Code ....⌘-Shift->
Outdent Code ....⌘-Shift-<

VIEW

Switch between Code and Design Views ....Ctrl-` (that's the ~ key)
Switch between Documents (Tabs).......................⌘-` (that's the ~ key)
Refresh Design View F5
Live View...Opt-F11

WORKING WITH DOCUMENTS & PANELS

Show/Hide Panels..F4
Switch to Next Document (Tab) ....⌘-` (that's the ~ key)
Switch to Previous Document (Tab) ....⌘-Shift-` (that's the ~ key)
Assets..Opt-F11
Behaviors...Shift-F4
Bindings...⌘-F10
Code Inspector..Opt-F10
Components ....⌘-F7
Databases ....⌘-Shift-F10
Files..F8
Frames...Shift-F2
AP Elements (Layers) F2
Properties ....⌘-F3
Reference Shift-F1
Results F7
Server Behaviors ....⌘-F9
Tag Inspector Opt-Shift-F9

MISC

Check Spelling..Shift-F7
Get File from Server ....⌘-Shift-D
Put File on Server..⌘-Shift-U

⬈NOBLE DESKTOP
<!--Exceptional computer graphics training.-->

594 Broadway, Suite 1202, New York, NY 10012
212.226.4149 www.nobledesktop.com